color recipes
for painted furniture
and **more**

color recipes
for **painted furniture**
and *more*

40 step-by-step projects to transform your home

annie sloan

CICO BOOKS
LONDON NEW YORK

Published in 2013
by CICO Books
An imprint of
Ryland Peters & Small Ltd
519 Broadway, 5th floor,
New York NY 10012
20–21 Jockey's Fields,
London WC1R 4BW

www.cicobooks.com

10 9 8 7 6 5 4 3 2

Text © Annie Sloan 2013
Design and photography © CICO Books 2013

Chalk Paint is a registered trademark of Annie Sloan Interiors Ltd.

A CIP catalog record for this book is available from the
Library of Congress and the British Library.

ISBN 978 1 908862 77 8

Printed in China

Managing editor: Gillian Haslam
Copy editor: Helen Ridge
Designer: Christine Wood
Photographer: Christopher Drake

RPS CICO BOOKS

For digital editions, visit
www.cicobooks.com/apps.php

contents

introduction

Over the years I have written many books, but this one is very personal as it charts the renovation of our farmhouse in northern France. Although we have owned the property for more than 20 years, over the past 12 months we have extended the house and redecorated throughout. This has given me a wonderful opportunity to experiment with new techniques (such as using my paint to dye fabrics) and the perfect excuse to buy more furniture from local markets and village fairs.

We chose the house because it is easy to get to from our home in Oxford. It takes an hour to reach the port on the south coast of England, and from there we catch the "midnight" ferry. After sleeping overnight on-board, we arrive in France in the early morning, with just another hour's drive ahead of us. The house is situated in the middle of the green and rolling Normandy countryside, an area renowned for its milk and cream, from the famous Normandy cows, and also for its apples.

There are orchards everywhere, and cider and calvados, the delicious apple brandy, are produced in abundance.

The house started as a retreat for the whole family, where the children could run about and do as they liked. We stayed there every summer, spending our days on the nearby beaches or in the surrounding countryside. The children played in the fields of tall maize and rode their bikes along the empty roads. They searched for glowworms, played in the tiny stream, made hideouts in the attics and sheds, and generally had a good time. We spent Christmases there, too, and even though it was very cold, we would soon warm up sitting by the big log fire and have tremendous fun.

The house is old. One of the beams in the kitchen has the date 1776 carved into the wood, although parts of the building may actually be older than that. On the ground floor, the walls are made of stone, with mud walls above, which was the

FAR LEFT *The farmhouse, built from stones with cob (mud and straw) walls, has other outbuildings which we currently use as storage. I particularly love this old oak door, and am planning to restore and reinstate the old fence.*

LEFT *The country kitchen is next to the Swedish-style room, so it was important to make certain that the styles flowed easily. I have taken a color from one room and used it in the next.*

RIGHT *Carved into one of the ceiling beams in the kitchen is the date 1776, the year that America gained her independence from Britain. Although this is a great age in itself, some parts of the house may be even older.*

traditional way to build houses all over Britain and Europe. The previous owners had tried their hand at modernization, and we spent ages removing the hardboard and plastic they had used to cover the ancient wooden beams, as well as scraping green gloss paint from the walls.

As the house is located in the heart of the French countryside, I chose to decorate it in a predominantly French rustic style. But, as you would imagine, I have also included other influences that continue to inspire me. When I decorate a room, I start with one large item of furniture as the pivotal piece against which everything else is measured. Smaller pieces are then added as I find them and the rooms are constantly evolving. I dress a room until it feels right, which is why you may notice curtains hanging at a window in one photograph but in another shot of the same room there are none.

I have divided the book into six chapters, with the first on how to use color and make up your own using my paints. This is followed by chapters on each of the decorating styles that are important to me: French Style, Boho Chic, Swedish Style, Country, and Modern Contemporary. I have broadly allocated a room for each of these styles but, naturally, there is some overlap, so you will find a Boho Chic painted chandelier in the Swedish room, for instance. Colors in one room will also feature in another. It is in this way that the rooms work together and always feel connected.

Annie Sloan

LEFT *All the furniture in this bedroom has been bought in France, although I see similar pieces all over the world. Scouring flea markets and visiting secondhand furniture stores for pieces to paint is great fun, and I'll continue to do this with the emphasis now on searching for paintings, prints, and the finishing touches.*

tools and materials

As you flick through the projects in this book, you'll see that none of them calls for specialist equipment. Have a few pots of paint in your chosen colors, some brushes, and clean rags to hand and you are all set to get started.

paint

The starting point is to choose the right paint for the job. This will make painting your furniture an enjoyable experience because the paint will be responsive and you will be able to work in a practical, flexible way. There are many house paints on the market, but I believe that my purpose-made paint, Chalk Paint® (see page 160 for stockists), is the best for the projects in this book. The paint has a very matte texture and absorbs wax easily, and has been specially created to be used in a huge variety of ways—for example, as a wash, with or without texture, or applied thickly. And one of the great bonuses with this paint is that there is no need to prime the furniture or rub it down in preparation, meaning you can start painting easily and quickly while you have the urge. The paint, despite being water based, even mixes easily with the solvent-based wax too, so you can color the final finish to get the exact color you want to achieve.

For the most part you only need to apply one coat of Chalk Paint®, but where two coats are necessary apply the first one with a big brush.

One of the most exciting and interesting ways to use the paint is on fabric. I used to do this many years ago, but have recently rediscovered this technique. One method is to use it as a dye by washing fabric in heavily diluted paint and the effect is wonderful— I have rewashed one dyed linen sheet several times now and the color has remained the same. The other method is to paint and then wax upholstered chairs with my paint, which creates a stunning effect.

brushes

Your brush does not have to be expensive, but it does need to have certain qualities because working with bad brushes can be very frustrating. I find that using a brush that is a mix of synthetic and bristle is the best. The hairs should be fairly long and flexible with a little bounce to allow you to be expressive in your work.

Have a collection of brushes to hand, such as a large one at least 3–4in (8–10cm) wide for painting onto the furniture with speed and a smaller 1–2in (2.5–5cm) brush to work paint into the intricate parts, such as moldings and corners. I tend to work with a 2in (5cm)

and 1in (2.5cm) brush. In some projects I recommend which brush to use, but it's more important to pick a size that feels comfortable for you to use and suits the size of the piece of furniture or wall/floor being worked on.

Don't choose brushes that are too short since the paint will not flow well, and don't use a brush with hard and inflexible bristles, because the paint will look scratchy. Don't have a floppy brush, because you will have to work too hard to make the paint spread.

I often mention artists' brushes—by this, I mean soft-haired ones from an artists' supplier. Cheap craft brushes will only result in frustration, as they are not responsive and the hairs quickly become floppy or fall out. The most expensive artists' brushes are made from sable hair, which are very good, although squirrel hair and high-quality synthetic brushes don't cost as much and work extremely well, offering the right amount of strength and spring. I use a range of artists' brushes: two flat-ended brushes, known as "one strokes," ¼in (6mm) and ½in (12mm) in size and made from high-quality synthetic hair; and two pointed brushes in a size 4 and a size 6, both made from sable hair.

wax, sandpaper, and varnish

I wax more or less everything I paint to get the right finish for my furniture and walls. I find it makes my projects strong and practical and gives them a beautiful, workable finish. I recommend that you choose a soft wax that can be applied easily with a brush. I often use a 1in (2.5cm) brush to apply wax, but you can use a large brush to get it done quickly if it feels more comfortable. After adding a layer of clear wax to a piece, you can then start applying dark wax or coloring the clear wax with some of my paint to alter the finish.

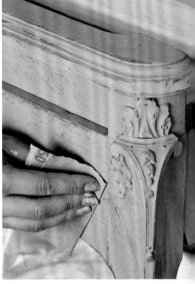

For the distressed look you need to be able to sand the waxed surface to reveal the wood or another coat of paint—have a range of fine, medium, and coarse sandpapers for this purpose. I tend to find using just the fine and medium grades is usually enough, but sometimes move onto the coarser paper if I really want to distress the furniture.

The only time I use varnish is on floors, when doing decoupage and transfer work, and when I use the crackle varnish set. I prefer to apply wax to my work at the end because it has such a soft finish, can be colored and changed as you work, and stops the work chipping.

cloths

Finally, have a good supply of clean, dry, lint-free cloths to hand so you can wipe brushes, polish wax, apply and wipe off paint, and generally use them to clean. I often buy old sheets from thrift stores and charity shops and find these are ideal.

working with paint colors

When working with color, I have always erred on the side of adventure and, as a result, I have made a lot of mistakes! However, that is the way we all learn, and the great advantage with paint is that it can be reapplied so easily. For some, working with color is an intuitive thing, while others are just too nervous to experiment and so play it safe with neutrals. Then there are those who are maybe just a little too daring at times and fall flat on their face!

If you wish to create your own colors, start out by mixing different paints together with your fingers on paper or making small quantities in a paint tray. Use teaspoons and half teaspoons of the different paints to create the desired color—is it a lot of white with a little bit of color or equal amounts? Once you have determined the ratio of colors, you can then go on to make larger quantities, using this as a guideline.

If you are painting a piece of furniture for a particular room, it might be a good idea to make up your paint colors in that room—the existing colors and the quality of the light can make a huge difference to how the paint will appear, and you may need to adjust your color mix to make it lighter or brighter or darker. One final thing, I always recommend that you paint in daylight. I have painted too many pieces in artificial light and then been horrified to see them in daylight—what I thought was a subtle blend of colors turned out to be an alarming mess!

understanding the color wheel

Mixing and combining paint is easily done if you know how color works, and for this a color wheel can be quite helpful. Use it as a springboard to launch you into an exciting mix of colors that you might previously have never considered.

A lot of color wheels that you will come across, though, are far too abstract and technical-looking and only serve to intimidate. For that reason, I have made my own for this book, using my paint colors. As you can see, there aren't a huge number of paints in my range. That's because by simply making them paler, darker, warmer, or cooler, it's possible to create an infinite number of colors.

The color wheel can be used in several ways:
• To darken a color—I rarely use black to make a color darker but, instead, add a complementary color, so the result is more stimulating, complex, and interesting.
• To find a color that will work next to or underneath another color.
• To make a color warmer or cooler.
• For inspiration!

The triangle of colors indicates the three primary colors which can't be mixed from other colors. Mix red and yellow together to make orange, mix yellow and blue together to make green, and mix blue and red together to make purple. I have placed my colors around this triangle of colors to show, for instance, that Old Violet is nearer to the blues than Emile.

Sometimes working with color is a simple matter of achieving balance. For example, lots of bright red and green in a room will be a terrible assault on the eyes, but the right soft tone of green with just a little scarlet could look sublime.

Finding a color's complementary color is simply a case of looking at the other side of the wheel at its "opposite" color. Facing English Yellow, for example, is Emile. Use a little Emile to darken English Yellow or use the two colors together but alter their tonal values by adding Old White. This means that you could have creamy pale yellows alongside lavender/lilac colors, although not in equal amounts.

If you want clashing colors, use adjacent primary and secondary colors, such as Emperor's Silk and Emile or Old Violet, or Emperor's Silk and Barcelona Orange. These colors can also be mixed together to adjust, for example, Emperor's Silk to make it more of a tomato red.

I have positioned my neutrals on the wheel with the colors they are most like, and opposite those they complement. Paris Grey, for example, has a blue tinge to it, so I have placed it with the blues, which are opposite the warm oranges and rust colors.

It is also possible with the color wheel to determine which three colors will work together. This goes by the rather grand name of a split complementary color scheme. It means that instead of using, say, the opposite color of Burgundy, which is Antibes Green, you could use the colors that are either side of it, which are Provence and Arles. The colors would not be used in equal quantities, of course, and not in the same tones either.

Mixing the three primary colors—red, blue and yellow—should, in theory, make black but in practice, because paints have white in them to increase covering power, browns are made rather than blacks. To make black you can use Burgundy, Aubusson Blue, and a touch of English Yellow.

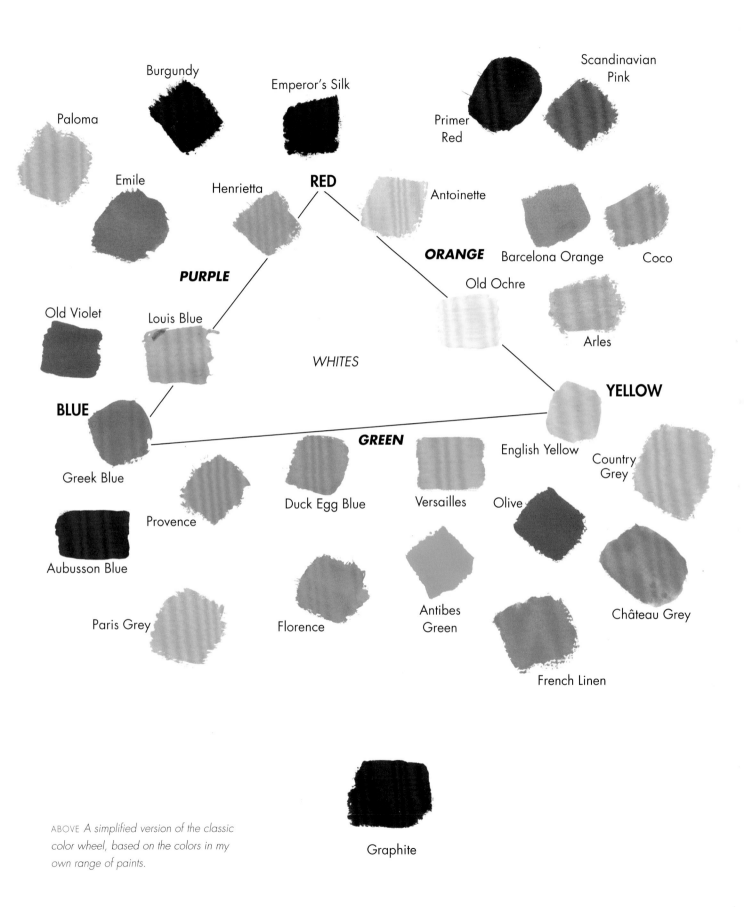

Burgundy

Emperor's Silk

Scandinavian Pink

Paloma

Primer Red

Emile

Henrietta

RED

Antoinette

Barcelona Orange

Coco

ORANGE

PURPLE

Old Ochre

Old Violet

Louis Blue

Arles

WHITES

YELLOW

BLUE

GREEN

English Yellow

Country Grey

Greek Blue

Duck Egg Blue

Versailles

Olive

Provence

Antibes Green

Château Grey

Aubusson Blue

Paris Grey

Florence

French Linen

Graphite

ABOVE *A simplified version of the classic color wheel, based on the colors in my own range of paints.*

red

Red is a primary color and one that projects forward, so a little goes a long way. Its range is quite large, covering orange-tinged tomato reds to deep plum, cherry, and aubergine reds. When we add white to reds, we create pinks, from salmon and strawberry pinks to cherry blossom pinks. In my range of paints, the scarlet red is Emperor's Silk, and the deep cherry is Burgundy, both classic colors. Henrietta is a rich complex pink. The complementary color to red is green, a cool secondary color, which can be added to reds and pinks to make them darker and deeper without losing any essential character.

Before the 18th century, the only reds available were the very expensive artist's pigment and the red oxides and ocher reds, which were a reddish brown. This color was used as a primer for many hundreds of years, as the earth pigment was so inexpensive and readily available. It is also a classic color to be used underneath gilding. This is my Primer Red. If you add white to these reds, however, you will have some beautiful dusty pinks—think of the dusky pinks of Venetian exteriors and the earthy pinks of traditional Swedish paintwork. Some of these ocher reds are tinged with an orange rust color because of the iron present in the soil from which they are made. Others even have a touch of purple in them caused by manganese in the soil. This is my Scandinavian Pink.

Bright reds first came to Europe in the 18th century via the red lacquer cabinets imported from the east, where cinnabar, the red pigment, was found more readily. A really bright red wasn't available as an interiors paint until the 20th century, which meant that pinks weren't either. In the 1960s, bright red paintwork became popular on furniture. To create that retro vintage look, use Emperor's Silk with just clear wax on top.

LEFT *The red of lacquered chinoiserie cabinets inspired me to make my Emperor's Silk paint. Used with gilding and some lightened Arles, which is a rich yellow, and covered with a dark wax, polished to a sheen, it creates a stunning effect.*

how to work with red

Emperor's Silk A pure bright red could be used on its own with dark wax for a strong Chinese lacquer red.

To make a more accurate Chinese lacquer color, mix Emperor's Silk (left) with Primer Red (bottom left).

Burgundy is a ruby cranberry-like color and can be used on neo-classical furniture or as an alternative to Chinese lacquer red.

Primer Red is also the color of Chinese lacquer and could be mixed with a little Barcelona Orange to make it a burnt orange.

colors that work with emperor's silk

Olive All the cooling green-grays (see below) combine well with all reds and pinks. The way to make green and red work together is to have one bright and one quiet. If both are bright, they will fight with each other.

Graphite and Paris Grey are as colorless as the reds are warm and lively so make a terrific contrast to each other. Use Emperor's Silk or Primer Red, then paint Graphite on top; distress a little for a striking Asian look.

Old Violet A great boho combination.

Cream looks retro with Olive and Louis Blue. Yellow and red are warm colors, so cool them by dirtying or making them darker. Primer Red looks good with Old Ochre, Burgundy, slightly lightened English Yellow, and lightened or deepened Emperor's Silk. Gold leaf also looks good on all reds, especially with dark wax.

making pinks

To make pinks: adding white to reds makes pinks. Adding Old White to Burgundy makes a dusty raspberry pink as Burgundy is nearer to blue on the color wheel.

You can get a really bright fuchsia pink by adding a little Old White to Emperor's Silk. The more white you add, the more it becomes strawberry pink.

making reds darker

To make Emperor's Silk or Burgundy less intense or darker, add a little of their complementary color. Here, Olive, a yellowish green, is added to Emperor's Silk to create a darker brownish red. If a little Olive is added to Burgundy, its opposite on the color wheel, the result is deep red.

Add a little Florence to Emperor's Silk to make a deeper color.

To make reds darker add just a little green. It has to be the green opposite on the color wheel otherwise you will make a brown.

the pinks Not all pinks are baby pink!

Henrietta is a slightly purplish pink, inspired by 18th-century rococo pinks and the painted neoclassical ceilings of Robert Adam. It works with Olive and Château Grey, as these cool, serious colors help to take the sweetness away from the pink. Henrietta is also a quirky boho color, good with Louis Blue and Versailles.

Scandinavian Pink is inspired by the traditional earthy pinks found in Swedish decorating. It makes the best "non-pink" because there is none of the baby girl pink to it.

Antoinette is a natural pink inspired by Marie Antoinette, but it's not too sweet so it can be used on a kitchen wall (see page 125) and not look like a bedroom.

Make reds warmer by adding, for instance, a touch of Barcelona Orange (right) to Emperor's Silk

cooling grays and greens These work particularly well with reds and pinks.

Château Grey with Old White creates sage greens and look good with bright reds.

Olive has a bit of ocher yellow in it. Adding Old White to it also makes sage greens.

Paris Grey works with pinks as well combined with Primer Red, Emperor's Silk, and Burgundy.

French Linen is a khaki color and looks terrific with Burgundy.

green

Green is a secondary color and it covers possibly the largest range of any color, as it displays so many different characteristics, ranging from sharp yellow lime greens, vivid grass greens, forest greens, and sea turquoise greens to coppery verdigris, copper greens, and earthy sage greens. Their personalities vary enormously, too—lime green, for example, is nothing like a bluish verdigris, yet they are both greens.

Red is the complementary color of green and a little of it can be added to green to make it darker. The two colors also work well side by side, provided that one of them is bright and the other dull and soft or pale. Generally, green is a cool color that recedes into the background, although the more yellow it is, the warmer it is and the more it seeks attention.

True, reliable greens for painting furniture came about in the 18th century when new pigments were invented—before that, greens were notoriously unreliable in the way they faded and darkened. The invention of Prussian green meant that true greens and a range of pale and clean greens could be made for the first time. Green started to be used on a scale never seen before. Chippendale, for example, designed and painted furniture for the 18th-century English actor David Garrick using cream with a deep green. With my Olive, Florence, and Antibes Green paints, together with Provence and Aubusson Blue, I have created a full range of greens.

Before the18th century, all over Europe, a green, earthy gray, similar to my Château Grey, was used for folk work and farmhouses. It was often made by mixing all the leftover paint from previous jobs, which resulted in a muddy green. In Sweden and Italy, the color of this earth pigment was particularly green but elsewhere it was more a green-tinged brown. Used next to a red or a pink, the green of the pigment was enhanced, but next to a true green, the color would, of course, look quite brown!

In the 19th and early 20th centuries, green became one of the most ubiquitous colors, as it was dependable, easily made, and still quite a new color, which made it fashionable. All over Europe, farmhouse furniture was painted in rich and deep greens. I often use Antibes Green with dark wax on top to re-create this color. The invention of a really bright blue green came in the 1930s, which made with eau de nil, a pale aqua blue green, when mixed with white and this is one of the colors which identifies the period.

LEFT *I particularly love old furniture that has been painted green because of the way the color ages. This early 19th-century English demi-lune cabinet has been painted and decorated with neoclassical motifs and a pastoral scene on the center panel. The green has faded, darkened, and bleached a little so it appears as a mix of deep olive greens and pale sage green with a hint of aquamarine. Touches of gold, soft whites, and pink lighten the overall effect.*

colors that work with olive mixes

Old Ochre A cool faded yellow.

Henrietta This sophisticated pink is the pale complementary color to Olive.

Burgundy A touch of elegant Burgundy is warming alongside a pale sage.

Duck Egg Blue This blue green looks wonderful with dark Olive, which brings out the blueness of the Duck Egg Blue.

how to work with olive

Olive

Olive and Florence make a medium moss or bottle green.

Versailles, an 18th-century soft, lightly yellowed dusky green, picks up other colors well and changes character accordingly.

Olive and Provence together make an eau de nil green, especially when a little Old White is added.

Château Grey is an elegant grayed green—the color found in French woodwork.

making greens lighter

Antibes Green with Old White makes a light color. Add a little English Yellow for lime greens.

Add Old White to Château Grey to make pale sage greens.

Add Old White to Florence to make it lighter.

making greens darker and cooler

Antibes Green and Florence make a cool clear mid green. This can also be achieved by using Aubusson Blue instead of Florence, resulting in forest greens. Add Old White to make spearmint greens.

Emperor's Silk added to Antibes Green gives a darker green.

Florence and Provence together make cool sea greens and aquas.

making greens warmer

Olive with English Yellow makes dirty lime greens.

English Yellow, Versailles, and Old White make warm yellow mossy greens.

colors that go with green

Primer Red Deep and warm, Primer Red works well with the grayness of Château Grey and Versailles.

Scandinavian Pink This traditional pink works well under Versailles and Château Grey.

Barcelona Orange works in a two-color technique with olive over the orange or as part of a retro combination.

Emile Try Emile inside an Olive painted cupboard.

blue

Blue is a primary color and generally cool, although the more purple it appears, which means that it's closer to red on the color wheel, the warmer it is. It has a lot of depth and recedes into the background, especially when it is dark and intensely colored. The range of blues extends from the greenish turquoise, pale aqua, and teal blues, through clear mid-sky blues and royal blues, to the purple end of the range with indigo and violet blues. Greens and blues can be quite difficult to differentiate, and opinion is often divided over whether certain blues are, in fact, greens.

Oranges and rusts combine well with blues, as they are their complementary colors and also warm. If the blue is bright, the complementary needs to be mellow and deep (Greek Blue with Primer Red). If the blue is mellow and deep, the complementary can be bright (Aubusson Blue with Barcelona Orange).

Blue is such a popular color now that it's surprising to learn that up until the late 18th century it was little used in decoration. Before then, it was difficult to make and didn't occur naturally, except as the very expensive pigment lapis lazuli and azurite. It was with the invention of Prussian blue in Germany that a dependable blue was first made, and blues became available for decoration generally. It was still very expensive, though, and its use was at first limited to the great palaces of Europe, notably in Sweden—Prussian blue has become synonymous with Swedish decoration—and at Charlottenburg Palace in Germany. My Aubusson Blue and Napoleonic Blue are similar to Prussian blue and can be used to make traditional colors for Swedish and neoclassical interiors. Combine them with Old White or Paris Grey to create mellow farmhouse gray blues. Duck Egg Blue and Louis Blue are perfect for the French and Swedish look, too.

Really bright and reliable electric blues became generally available in the 20th century. Provence and Greek Blue are modern blues but they also suit retro and country interiors. Use them as they are, dark waxed, or with Old White for a faded rustic look.

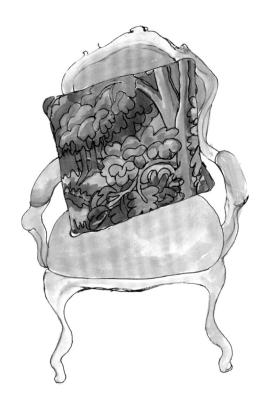

LEFT *Aubusson Blue is named after a small town in central France, famous for its tapestry making. The color traditionally used to make the tapestries is a very distinctive deep, cool blue. Fine cushions are made from a piece of tapestry featuring the deep various blues.*

how to work with aubusson blue Recreating classic 18th-century blues

Aubusson Blue (top) and Provence (bottom) make a mellow teal blue (center). Because Provence has white in it, adding it to Aubusson Blue makes a soft green blue.

Aubusson Blue (top) and Florence (bottom) make a clear teal blue (center). Add a little Florence to Aubusson Blue to take it nearer to green

Aubusson Blue (top) with Old White makes a teal blue. Lighten Aubusson Blue with Old White to make a range of blues. The white will bring out the greenish character of the color.

Aubusson Blue mixed with Country Grey gives a stormy gray, Swedish blue.

Mix Aubusson Blue (top) with Louis Blue (below) to soften Aubusson.

making pale blues

Provence plus Old White makes make a aquamarine.

Louis Blue (left) and Old White (below) makes a soft mid-blue. then add Provence (right) with Old White (below) makes a pale robin's egg blue.

Greek Blue mixed with Old White makes a fresh sky blue.

Add Louis Blue (left) to Duck Egg Blue and Old White to make gray blues.

making warmer blues

Aubusson Blue, Burgundy, and Old White combined make a purple-tinged pink.

Aubusson Blue mixed with Burgundy makes a deep aubergine.

Old Violet (left), Louis Blue (right), and Old White make lilac blues.

making darker blues

To make blues darker, mix a little of the complementary which is Barcelona Orange or Primer Red. Greek Blue with Primer Red, brings out a purple tinge to the color because there is little red in Greek Blue and Primer Red

Barcelona Orange mixed with Greek Blue makes a gray, which is either cooler or warmer, depending on the ratio of the mixture that is brought out with the addition of Old White.

Arles (right) with Aubusson Blue (left) creates a gray mossy color.

Provence (left) and Antibes Green (right) make a greeny turquoise.

colors that work with blues

Primer Red This warm, rust-colored deep orange works well with the coolness of blues. Barcelona Orange is a bright alternative.

Scandinavian Pink Aubusson Blue and Scandinavian Pink is a combination used in traditional Swedish interiors.

Château Grey Soft and cool, Château Grey works with the brilliance of Florence.

Antibes Green has a modern look combined with the strong blues.

yellow

Yellow is a primary color with the smallest range of colors within it—from just earthy mustard yellow to mid- and lemon yellow. These are all distinctly yellow in character, too, unlike the greens, which contain a huge range of different characters. Yellow is generally a warm color, but lemon yellow, which is nearer to the green end of yellow on the color wheel, is cold and crisp and lacking in depth. It needs to be used carefully so that it's not drowned or doesn't make other colors look acid. Lemon yellow can also appear green at night, which is why I prefer to use my English Yellow (see below) instead, which has no black in it. (Mixing lemon yellow with black results in an olive green and with electric lights the green is all too apparent.)

Yellow, generally, can be difficult to use because it doesn't have much strength. It is a color that projects forward but not as much as red. Pale yellow can be weak and is easily drowned out, which makes it difficult to find a color to partner it. Yellow at its brightest needs Graphite to show it up and create a good contrast. Its complementary color is purple, and the way to darken yellow is to add purple, rather than black, which tends to turn it green. Creamy yellows and lavender together look very pretty.

The earth pigment yellow ocher is found in abundance in many countries and, being relatively inexpensive, it has traditionally been used on the exterior of houses, as well as on furniture and woodwork. My yellow ocher, called Arles, is quite bright, so it can be darkened, lightened, and muted. Named after the town in the south of France, Arles is the earthy end of yellow, a color synonymous with farmhouses all over the world and with the Mediterranean in particular, where many walls are painted earthy yellows and whites, with shutters and doors in various shades of blue green.

Chinese hand-painted wallpaper in the 17th and 18th centuries featured a yellow that probably inspired the creation of chrome yellow, which was first produced in the early 19th century. It came to be used on the smartest drawing room walls in London, as well as on furniture. My version of it is English Yellow, so-called because of the original color's popularity in English drawing rooms. When lightened with Old White, a soft, creamy, pale yellow is created.

English Yellow can be used to paint both modern and classic furniture. For an elegant, neoclassical look, pair English Yellow walls with Graphite furniture. But for a retro 1950s look, use English Yellow either in its pure form or lightened to make pretty primrose colors. Alternatively, use Cream, which is a pale yellow, with Paris Grey.

LEFT *Outcrops of the earth pigment yellow ocher can be found all over the world and, being so readily available and therefore inexpensive, it has traditionally been used to paint the walls of houses. Inspired by this, I made my Arles paint in homage to the town in Provence where Van Gogh painted, near the hills of Roussillon where the pigment is mined. Many of the houses nearby are painted in a sunny array of mellow yellows.*

colors that work with earthy yellows

Old Violet, with a little Old White, makes lavender, the perfect Provençal combination.

Olive with Old White makes a dusty pale olive, also perfect for the south of France.

Duck Egg Blue, Provence, pale Antibes Green, Louis Blue, and Versailles are all colors used for shutters in the Mediterranean and other places with a similar climate.

Old Ochre is a cool, faded, pale yellow ocher.

how to darken yellows

Add Emile, its complementary, to darken English Yellow rather than Graphite as this will result in a green-tinged yellow.

To darken Arles, use a tiny amount of Emile.

how to lighten yellows

English Yellow and Old White together make a pretty pale primrose for classic painted furniture.

Lighten Arles with Old White to make soft, natural, honey-colored yellows.

how to make warm yellows

English Yellow with Burgundy makes, I think, a very warm sunrise yellow.

Mix English Yellow and Barcelona Orange to make a mellow sunrise yellow.

English Yellow and Arles together make a lovely warm, vintage 1950s yellow.

Mix Barcelona Orange and Arles for a mandarin yellow.

Mix Primer Red and Arles to make gingery ochers.

how to make cool yellows

To make lime green, mix English Yellow and Antibes Green, with a tiny amount of white to pull the color out. Mixing English Yellow with a little Antibes Green gives a perfect vintage lime color.

Mix English Yellow with Louis Blue and a little Old White to make a mellow, classic distressed grayed yellow.

colors that work with english yellow

Paris Grey A cool bluish gray.

Paloma Made by mixing yellow, purple, and Old White, Paloma naturally looks good with English Yellow.

Olive and yellow together can be difficult but the depth of Olive is perfect with English Yellow.

Burgundy with a touch of lightened English Yellow is sumptuous and neo-classical.

gray

Grays and neutrals can sound a little unexciting, yet they are probably the most important tools in the world of color. Choosing the exact tone and variation of a neutral can make all the difference to a painted piece. White alone can sometimes be too stark and needs other colors to make it more at one with the base coat, so that it doesn't stand out too much.

Neutrals have always been with us, of course, but some of the more interesting ones are those that became popular in the 18th century when colors were limited. Raw and burnt umber earth pigments, which were inexpensive, mixed with the newly invented but expensive Prussian blue and white, made a very pretty blue gray. Neutrals were traditionally made by the

painter and decorator mixing all the paint leftovers together, then adding white to achieve interesting tones and nuances. My Château Grey is inspired by this old mix as well as by terre verte, a greenish earth pigment. Old White is my standard white, cool and soft, which I based on a color I first noticed in old paintwork.

The easiest way to make grays is by mixing white and black together, but this doesn't give you really interesting colors with depth and interest. The best results come from mixing two complementary colors, that is, colors that are opposite each other on the color wheel. The theory behind this is that the three primary colors—red, blue, and yellow—mixed together should make black. In practice, however, these colors may already have some white in them, meaning that they are not perfect primaries, and so the end result won't be a perfect black. If the paints are not perfect complementaries, then the resulting color mix will be a brown rather than a black or gray. Adding some white to the mixed color is how the delicate brown or grayness of the color is achieved. Mixing complementaries and near complementaries, then adding white, opens up a world of delicate neutrals.

My Paris Grey and Paloma paints are grays made from complementaries (see below). Paloma will look wonderful with rich purples or creams because they make a connection with the colors in the paint.

Grays in all forms, whether dark and charcoal-like or with a hint of blue or brown, are synonymous with Swedish interiors. Gray is also used in minimal and retro interiors.

LEFT *Swedish dressers and secretaires are often painted on the outside in soft grays, with the inside in earthy pinks, like Scandinavian Pink, or soft blue greens, such as Duck Egg Blue or Louis Blue.*

colors that work with gray

Duck Egg Blue This is a grayed blue so works well with whites and very pale grays but particularly with Graphite.

Old White This also works well with gilding (see Gilded Mirror, page 48).

Aubusson Blue—a Swedish combination.

Scandinavian Pink Scandinavian Pink with grays is another typical Swedish combination

neutrals

Paris Grey Made by mixing orange and blue.

French Linen Inspired by old French paintwork and, like Château Grey, by the paint mixes traditionally made by combining leftovers and terre verte pigment.

Graphite Like my Old White, Graphite, which is almost black, is not a simple, hard color but a mellow, sophisticated mix. It can be darkened with dark wax or used over Aubusson Blue to make it deeper.

Paloma Made by mixing purple and yellow.

Country Grey and Old White Country Grey is made from white and raw umber pigment resulting in a cool, pale brown/gray.

mixing complementaries Mixed complementaries to make grays and browns

Primer Red and Florence Opposite colors on the color wheel, Primer Red is an earthy, slightly orange red, while Florence is a bluish green. Neither contains much white, so when mixed together, the result is a very dark, brown black. Adding Old White to the mix gives a warm, astrakhan gray.

Old Violet and Arles together make a warm gray. With the addition of Old White, you have a mellow gray.

Barcelona Orange mixed with Greek Blue makes a gray, which is either cooler or warmer, depending on the ratio of the mixture that is brought out with the addition of Old White.

Emperor's Silk mixed with Antibes Green makes a brown, rather than a gray, because Antibes is rather yellowish. With the addition of white, a pale mushroom color is created.

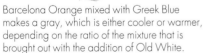

Burgundy and Antibes Green Burgundy is a blue-red, and Antibes Green a yellow-green. When mixed together, the stronger red pigment takes over, giving a rich, purple-tinged brown. Adding Old White brings out the softness and interesting pink tones.

Emile and Arles mixed together make a warm brown.

french style

Think of French interiors and images of monogrammed linens, expressively carved armoires, glittering chandeliers, and scenic toile de Jouy fabric probably spring to mind. The French have a design style that is unique and delightfully decorative but with a certain restraint, where less is decidedly more.

French style has had a profound influence on decoration the world over. Eighteenth-century rococo is what many see as quintessentially French and, although Napoleon later brought in a more rigid style, curves and playfulness are still never far away in French decoration. These style ideas were taken up all over Europe and made their way to America and the rest of the world, although usually adapted in some small way.

For me, French style is a complex mix of over 200 years of various influences—political, cultural, and geographical. With such diversity, it's difficult to pin down one look but that's partly what makes the whole subject so fascinating. I have two interpretations of French style, from two distinct traditions: the grand château, as epitomized by Versailles, and practical rural farm life. I have plucked elements from both for my Normandy home but as the house was originally an old farm, rustic pieces suit it well and I have not been able to make it too grand. However, there is a suggestion, perhaps, that I may have raided a château for my bedroom!

At first, I thought that the style of this bedroom would be Swedish-inspired, but the room had other ideas and it started to become French in style. My husband found a beautiful little etching of a French ship (see page 55, Painted Lamp Base) in the right colors and with a little fluttering French flag. The room now is basically white with blue, but I introduced elements of Burgundy in the pictures and on the painted furniture.

Choosing the right color palette is vital to create a French interior. Lots of whites are essential, of course. Aubusson Blue, French Linen, Château Grey, Antoinette, and Burgundy also work well. For something more neoclassical and Napoleonic, try Versailles, Louis Blue, Duck Egg Blue, and Cream as well as strong colors, such as Florence.

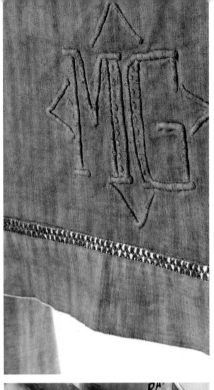

gilded rococo chair

Inspired by Madame de Pompadour, mistress of Louis XV, and her love of comfort, this elegant chair couldn't be anything else but French. The original 18th-century design has been reproduced ever since in a variety of shapes: with oval or shield backs; with padded arms or no arms; with filled-in caned or upholstered arms. Some have a double cushion and filled-in sides; some are upholstered, some caned. They are variously called bergère chairs or fauteuils, which is French for armchair. What all the designs have in common is their carved and decorated surrounds, often with flower or shell shapes. My chair is rococo in inspiration, with its cabriole legs and curvy shape. Later chairs are more classic in design, with straight legs.

Certain colors suit this style of chair very well: Aubusson Blue, inspired by the sumptuous rococo colors of the French Aubusson rugs; pale blues, such as Louis Blue and Duck Egg Blue; Antoinette, a soft pink; and, of course, Whites and Greys. If you wanted to apply three coats of paint, then choose Primer Red as the first coat, which is traditional under gilding. A little of it peeking through looks very opulent.

YOU WILL NEED
- Aubusson Blue paint
- Duck Egg Blue paint
- Round bristle brush, No. 8
- Water-based gold size
- Fine, soft-haired brush, to apply the gold size
- Brass leaf
- Dry, firm but soft-haired brush, to push down the brass leaf
- Clean, dry, lint-free cloth, to apply the shellac
- Clear shellac
- Clear wax
- 1in (2.5cm) brush, to apply the wax

1 Paint the wood of the chair in Aubusson Blue, adding a little water to the paint if it doesn't go on easily. You can either remove the upholstery first or you can paint over the fabric, as I did, poking the brush under the fabric where you need to.

2 Look at the carving on the chair and work out where you want to apply the leaf. It could be all over the chair or just in parts, as I have done. Paint on the gold size with the fine, soft-haired brush, working it into all the crevices. Leave the size to become completely clear.

3 Take either the whole sheet of brass leaf or part of a sheet and hold it with one hand. With the other hand, use a dry, firm but soft-haired brush to push the leaf onto the sized areas. Brush it firmly to make sure it is stuck. Use the brush to push the leaf into the crevices. Brush away all the excess leaf. If you find that you have any gaps, you may want to repeat this step after re-applying the size.

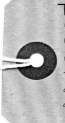

Tip: When gold size is first applied, it looks white, but it quickly changes to a luminous violet color before becoming clear. This takes approximately five minutes, depending on the air temperature and how thickly it is applied. From then on, it is ready to use at any time, as it remains sticky indefinitely, although the stickiness does decrease with time.

4 Make a pad from a piece of the cloth and dab the shellac onto the gilding and lightly wipe all over. This will protect the gilding so make certain that you cover it thoroughly.

5 Paint all over with Duck Egg Blue, wiping it off with a dry cloth and repainting as you go, to achieve the desired amount of distressing.

6 Once the paint is dry, apply a layer of clear wax all over the wood with the 1in (2.5cm) brush, to protect it.

7 Re-upholster the chair. Mine has been covered in a classic toile de Jouy fabric with single piping and upholstery studs.

LEFT *If you can't find the right shade of fabric, you could "dye" it with paint (see page 36). Colors that would work particularly well are shown here, from left to right: Emperor's Silk, Emile, French Linen, Florence, Duck Egg Blue, and Barcelona Orange. Some of these colors are stronger than others, such as Emperor's Silk, which will take to the fabric very easily.*

ABOVE *Parts of the top layer of Duck Egg Blue have been rubbed away with a dry cloth in places to reveal the darker Aubusson Blue underneath and the gilding, giving the chair a more natural, aged appearance.*

distressed armoire

Inspired by the Swedish take on French style in the 18th century, this classically shaped and designed armoire has been painted using exactly the same technique as the bedside table, shown in the step-by-step instructions overleaf.

I used French Linen, which is a dark gray, then brushed on a layer of clear wax. Over this, I added a second, paler coat made from a mix of Paris Grey and Old White, thinned down with water. Before the paint was completely dry, I brushed on another layer of clear wax, wiping it over with a clean, dry cloth to create a washed, dragged, and distressed effect.

ABOVE *I painted over and waxed the rather shiny brass hinges. Wiping them straight afterward with a cloth removed some of the paint and wax, so that patches of metal were revealed, creating a wonderfully uneven effect.*

ABOVE *I painted the inside of the armoire Greek Blue, which is a bright, clear, and fairly strong color. Remember that an interior like this is in shadow so usually a color with a bit of punch works better than one that is subtle and dark.*

YOU WILL NEED

- French Linen paint
- Paris Grey paint
- Old White paint
- Greek Blue paint, for inside the armoire
- Medium oval bristle brush
- Clear wax
- Small wax brush
- Plenty of clean, dry, lint-free cloths
- Paint roller tray
- Medium flat bristle brush

The bedside table shown in these steps (and featured in the photograph of the lamp base project on page 54) was painted in the same colors as the armoire on the previous page and using the same dragging technique.

LEFT *Having painted the armoire in French Linen, I covered it in a diluted mix of Paris Grey and Old White (see step 4). Before applying the color, I tested it on paper to make sure that it was light enough to show up on the French Linen background when dry. After brushing on the paint, wiping it away with a clean, dry cloth as I went, I immediately waxed the armoire all over, as I did for the bedside table.*

1 Remove the drawer, then turn the table upside down. Using the medium oval bristle brush, apply French Linen paint fairly smoothly in all directions. Paint the drawer separately. Let the paint dry.

Tip: If you can, turn a piece of furniture upside down before painting it. This way you won't miss areas such as the underside of molding and the awkward ends of the feet. You will also finish with the piece the right way up!

2 Turn the table back up the right way. Continue painting with the French Linen until everywhere is covered, and finish by brushing in the direction of the wood. It is not essential for the paint to look too smooth. Let the paint dry.

3 After the paint has dried, brush on a layer of clear wax. Work in small sections at a time, applying a fresh coat of wax as you go and making sure the whole piece is covered. The wax should not be too thick but it doesn't matter if it isn't completely worked in—it should be a little "sticky." Remove any excess wax with a clean, dry cloth.

4 Mix roughly equal measures of Paris Grey and Old White together in a paint roller tray. Dilute it with enough water so that the paint flows really easily and becomes a little translucent. Working in small sections at a time, spread the diluted mix over the wax with the flat bristle brush, to make a thin translucent wash. The paint needs to be applied, then wiped off immediately afterward (see step 5).

5 With plenty of clean, dry cloths to hand, wipe off the paint gently, spreading it over a larger area than your initial brushed area, to leave a stripy wash of paint. Paint then wipe in two areas at a time, such as the side of the cabinet, then the front, and so on, until you achieve a beautiful dragged effect.

dyeing fabric with paint

My elderly neighbor in Normandy, Marie Gaillard, moved to a retirement home and no longer wanted her old linen. Luckily for me, none of her family did either, so I very gladly bought it. I now have a huge pile of gorgeous linen, all of it white and much of it monogrammed, including one very pretty piece that belonged to Marie's mother.

I have used this linen on beds and upholstery, and also for curtains. Not wishing to have white everywhere, I decided to dye the linen for these curtains with Aubusson Blue paint. I left them unlined so that the light would filter through, which emphasized the texture of the fabric and the slight unevenness of the "dye." According to tradition, when Marie was married, all the sheets in her trousseau were embroidered with her initials, "MG." This simple monogram takes pride of place in the center of the pelmet.

The intensity of the final color depends on the ratio of paint to water, the shade of paint, the type of fabric, and the amount of it being dyed. Old French linen sheets are often particularly large, so work well as curtains. My linen sheet measured 10 x 7¼ft (3 x 2.2m). To dye it, I used about one-third of a liter can of paint and approximately 7.5 liters (15½ pints) of water. Any material that is coated or containing polyester will not take the dye so well.

YOU WILL NEED
- Aubusson Blue paint
- Water
- White linen sheet
- Large, old metal tub
- Wooden stick, for stirring
- Rubber gloves (optional)

1 Pour the paint carefully into the tub—I did this in the yard where it didn't matter if the "dye" was spilled. Gently mix in the water (in a ratio of roughly 1 part paint to 20 parts water, but you can adjust this ratio depending how light or dark you wish the "dye" to be) with the stick. Leave the sheet to soak for about 30 minutes.

2 Remove the sheet from the tub and hang it outdoors to drip dry. You can then wash it in a machine or leave it as it is.

3 Once the sheet is dry, make up the curtains according to the size of your window. If the sheet is monogrammed, you can cut off the embroidered end of the sheet and turn it into a pelmet.

LEFT *After making up the curtains, I experimented with washing a remnant of the dyed blue fabric with other pieces of linen. The result was a delightful and delicately washed-out blue. I also dyed one of the sheets using Scandinavian Pink, which gave this wonderful dusty pink color.*

RIGHT *Summer daisies and sweet-smelling honeysuckle grow wild in the hedgerows in Normandy. Arranged in an earthenware pitcher (jug), they are offset beautifully by these vintage linen curtains dyed in Aubusson Blue.*

wax-resist bed

I found this wonderful bed, with its low footboard and elegantly understated headboard, in France. Its size and shape were perfect for the room I had earmarked for it, and the low footboard meant that it didn't get in the way of the light coming in through the single window.

The bed also suited the existing furniture in style. The first piece I had painted for the room was the large armoire in French Linen and Greek Blue (see page 32), but this was quite dark and I needed the bed to be a lighter color, so the room wouldn't appear gloomy. My blue-painted bergère chair (see page 28) was also in this room.

Even though the bed was rather elegant, I wanted to give it a soft, lightly textured country look that wouldn't be at odds with the very rustic wall behind the headboard, which was painted in Old White. I decided to try an old technique using a wax candle to make a resist for the paint, where the textured effect would be obvious but not overly distressed.

YOU WILL NEED

- Aubusson Blue paint
- Greek Blue paint
- Duck Egg Blue paint
- Old White paint
- Paint roller tray
- No. 8 or 12 brush
- Wax candle
- Clean, dry, lint-free cloths
- Coarse sandpaper
- Clear wax
- Brush, for applying the wax

LEFT *The color theme in the room had already evolved into mainly blues and whites. To develop this further, I chose three tones of blue for the bed—Aubusson Blue, Greek Blue, and Duck Egg Blue— painting on the darkest first and finishing with the palest.*

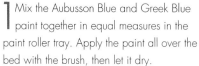

1 Mix the Aubusson Blue and Greek Blue paint together in equal measures in the paint roller tray. Apply the paint all over the bed with the brush, then let it dry.

2 Rub the wax candle hard over the wood, using its length as well as its pointy end. Wherever there is wax, the next layer of paint will not stick. Wipe away any loose wax with a clean, dry cloth.

3 Paint over the Aubusson Blue and Greek Blue mix with a coat of Duck Egg Blue. Let it dry.

4 Rub the wax candle over the wood here and there, where you want a more textured effect. Remove any loose wax with a cloth.

5 Rub the wood lightly all over with coarse sandpaper to reveal patches of darker blue underneath. The sandpaper will also give a slightly scratchy look.

6 Rub the candle again all over the wood, including over the areas where the darker blue color is coming through.

7 Mix one part of Duck Egg Blue with four parts of Old White in a clean roller tray, then brush on a coat of the paint all over the wood. Let it dry.

8 Rub the wood all over with coarse sandpaper, using strong and light pressure, to reveal the two different paint colors underneath.

9 Apply a coat of clear wax with either the brush or a clean, dry cloth. Wipe away any excess wax with a cloth.

RIGHT *The wax-resist technique works extremely well on the elegant headboard and complements the rustic wall behind, which has been painted in Old White.*

chipped paint cabinets

The appeal of old paint lies in its uneven patina, the varied and subtle coloring, and the way in which it may have become chipped and cracked over the years. At a time when so much of what we have in our lives is a carbon copy of what everyone else has, the attaction of a uniquely aged object is undeniable.

Painting this matching pair of rather dull and fairly recent reproduction bedside cabinets and then chipping the paint, to give the appearance of aging, has completely transformed them. As a point of interest, you will never find a matching pair of antique French bedside cabinets—there is always a large one for the gentleman, which would probably have contained the chamber pot, and a smaller, daintier one for the lady.

This entire room is a mix of cool blues, grays, and whites, which I felt needed a little lift. I achieved this by adding warmth to the pale Country Grey cabinets with a narrow decorative line around the top of the ledge and around the drawer front, painted in diluted Burgundy.

YOU WILL NEED

- Old White paint
- Country Grey paint
- Burgundy paint, for the fine, decorative line
- Medium oval brush
- Clear shellac (optional)
- Hairdryer
- Very coarse sandpaper
- ½in (12mm) flat brush, to apply the wash
- No. 4 flat artist's brush (sable is best, but expensive), to paint the cabinet-top line
- Clean, dry, lint-free cloths
- No. 4 pointed artist's brush, to paint the Burgundy line
- Clear wax
- 1in (2.5cm) brush, to apply the wax

1 Leave the can of Old White open at least overnight (see also Tip, below) so that the paint thickens. It should be of a consistency that will not drip from the brush.

Tip: Instead of leaving the lid off the paint overnight in order for it to thicken, speed up the process by leaving the can with its lid on in the fridge for about 2 hours (the time will depend on how thick the paint is to begin with).

2 Turn the cabinet upside down and paint a first coat of thickened Old White all over with the oval brush. Turn the cabinet the right way up and apply a coat of paint everywhere else. If any unattractive stains come through from the original wood finish, apply a coat of clear shellac (see Tip, below).

3 Lay the paint on very thickly in different directions and in varying thicknesses over the first coat, particularly over the top and along the edges of the cabinet and where you would like to create some chipping. For me, this was the raised lip of the cabinet, the front of the legs, and a little bit of the drawer. In a few areas, I applied three or four layers of paint to create a particularly chipped look.

4 Wherever the paint is especially thick, such as on the top of the cabinet and the fronts of the legs, use a hairdryer to dry it and make it crack. Start off by holding the dryer very close to the paint, to warm it up, then move it away slightly as cracks start to appear after a minute or so. This will stop the paint from bubbling. If cracks don't appear, apply another coat of paint and repeat. Applying the paint in different directions and in varying thicknesses in step 3 means that the cracks will run in different directions and vary in size (the thicker the paint, the wider the crack), producing a varied crackled effect, which looks more natural.

Tip: To block a stain coming through the paint from the original wood finish—this usually only occurs on pieces made in the mid-20th century—brush on a coat of clear shellac, which will dry almost on impact. Add another coat of paint to cover the stain.

5 Fold the sandpaper in half to give a hard edge, then nick the edges of the cabinet, so that the paint chips off, revealing the wood beneath. Sand any other areas that you want to appear chipped. Areas that have been dried with the hairdryer will be very hard and therefore more difficult to sand. You will need to apply more pressure for these to look worn.

6 Mix the Country Grey with enough water to make a very translucent, subtle, and uneven watercolor "stain." Brush the diluted paint over the top of the cabinet with the small flat brush, gently wiping it away with a clean, dry cloth as you go. This is a gentler way of bringing out the crackles than using dark wax. Wherever there are cracks, the paint will gather.

7 Add some more Country Grey to the watercolor "stain" to thicken it, then paint a freehand line around the cabinet top, a suitable distance in from the edge, using the width of the flat artist's brush. When painting a decorative line like this, take care to give it enough breathing space so that it doesn't look squashed, and ensure that the rectangle you make is a pleasing shape.

8 To accentuate the worn look, use a clean, dry cloth to wipe away parts of the line or, at least, soften it. This will also allow you to straighten the line where it may look a bit too wobbly.

9 Dilute the Burgundy paint with some water so that it is a pinky color and almost translucent, then paint a soft line around the top of the ledge and around the drawer front with the pointed artist's brush. Vary the intensity of the color, and dab and wipe away the paint with a cloth in some areas, to give a more natural look.

10 Once the paint is completely dry, brush clear wax over the cabinet, a small area at a time. Use a clean, dry cloth to remove any excess.

Tip: I usually wax before sanding but for this project, and for the French kitchen chairs (see page 120), I have done the opposite. This creates a more robust and obviously worn look.

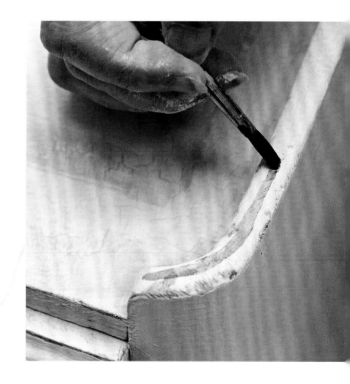

gilded mirror

This huge mirror was originally the door of an armoire—you can still see the keyhole. I have painted it in the timeless, classical look of the Palace of Versailles, where the wooden paneling is painted white with gilded moldings and carvings. The Napoleon III Apartments in the Louvre in Paris have similar paneling with chandeliers, and the rooms glitter with light and sparkle. This is a very inspiring look, but a little goes a long way in my mud-walled farmhouse room!

My Old White paint was inspired by the white of these historic rooms. Matte, neutral, and slightly cool in color, it works perfectly with gilding, which is reflective and warm. Traditionally, gilding is applied over a reddish-brown, ocher-red earth color called bole, and this is the color of my Primer Red paint. I have used brass leaf, which is an economical method of achieving a gilded look—you can use real gold but this would be in the form of transfer leaf and is, of course, more costly. Unlike gold, brass needs to be sealed with wax because it will tarnish as it oxidizes.

YOU WILL NEED

- Old White paint
- Primer Red paint
- 2in (5cm) synthetic flat brush
- Clear shellac (optional)
- Plenty of clean, dry, lint-free cloths
- Small (No. 6) artist's brush
- Gold size
- Loose brass leaf
- Dry, firm but soft-haired brush, to push down the brass leaf
- Clear wax

1 Paint the wood with Old White using a flat brush, working with the grain of the wood so there are few brush marks. You may need to add a little water to the paint to achieve this.

2 If any yellowish-brown stain comes through the paint from the wood, apply a coat of clear shellac with a cloth (see page 46). I used dark shellac for this photograph so it could be clearly seen.

3 Paint over the shellac with Old White and let it dry.

4 Using the small artist's brush, paint the molded areas in Primer Red. The molding between the mirror and the frame is most important, as this gives the feeling of reflected light. Allow to dry.

5 Apply gold size over the Primer Red using the (cleaned) small artist's brush (see page 80).

6 Apply the brass leaf over the gold size, using the soft-haired brush to push and guide the leaf into the moldings and awkward sections. Tear off small pieces of leaf to cover the whole area. If you want a very solid gold color, paint on a second coat of size and add more brass leaf.

7 Using a clean, dry cloth, apply clear wax over the brass leaf and the paintwork. If you want your paintwork to remain completely matte, avoid buffing or restrict the wax to the brass leaf.

transfer image

Instead of having to paint an image on a piece of furniture or use decoupage, it is now possible to directly transfer an image using transfer printing. With this method, the image remains on the furniture but the paper it is on is removed. It is very easy to do. Before transferring the image, I painted my side table with Old White, then left it to dry completely. It's important not to apply any wax beforehand.

A transfer image can come from almost anywhere, such as a decoupage motif book, a magazine, or the internet. The picture can then be adjusted to fit, scanned, and printed using a computer. This technique works best with laser prints and photocopies. The ink in inkjet prints can cause the image to bleed from time to time, which might look a little messy.

LEFT *The image I chose of a fine classical woman wearing a laurel wreath, which represents victory, came from a book of copyright-free images—the copyright issue is only important if you are going to sell to others. I made the print in black and white because the image would be sharper and it suited the neoclassical side table that was to go in my bedroom in France. In the background of the main picture, you can see a vintage French screen covered in sepia-colored toile de Jouy.*

YOU WILL NEED

- Chosen image
- Computer, scanner, printer, photocopier (as appropriate)
- Sharp scissors
- All-in-one Annie Sloan Decoupage Glue & Varnish
- 1in (2.5cm) brush, to apply decoupage medium
- Pin (optional)
- Damp sponge or cloth (optional)
- Clean, dry, lint-free cloths
- Clear wax
- Medium sandpaper

Tip: When choosing your image, remember that it will transfer in reverse, so you may need to flip it on your computer before printing it out, especially if any text is included.

1 Size your chosen image on a computer or a
photocopier, then print it out. I made three copies in
total, flipping two of them so that two faces turn toward
each other on the side table, as shown in the photograph,
and the third image, not visible, looks toward the front. Cut
around the images with a sharp pair of scissors, getting as
close to the edge of the design as possible—excess white
around the edges makes life harder later.

2 Brush a thin, even layer of the decoupage medium over the part
of the side table that you will be covering with the transfer. Try to
keep the area of glue on the furniture as close in size to the image
as possible—the glue has a slight sheen and could leave a shiny
area around your transfer. Then place your image right side up on
a clean work surface, and brush on a thin, even layer of glue,
making sure that you don't get any glue on the unprinted side of the
image.

3 While the image is still wet with the glue, position it
carefully, face down. It may help to almost roll the
image flat from one edge or work outward from the
middle, dispersing any trapped air bubbles as you go.
If there are any air bubbles that refuse to budge, gently
prick them with a pin. Once the image is in place, gently
rub it with a clean, dry cloth to make sure it is totally stuck
to the surface. Pay special attention to the edges! Allow
to dry completely.

4 Once the glue has completely dried, wet the image a little with your fingers, then gently rub it in a circular motion, to start removing the paper. Alternatively, use a sponge or cloth. Once you've rubbed off the first layer, the image will still look very cloudy when dry. Continue wetting and rubbing off the paper until the image seems very clear. Be aware, though, that it will look a little dull when dry.

5 When completely dry, apply clear wax over the transfer image with a clean, dry cloth, and the remaining paper will become translucent. The dull remaining film of paper should become clear and your image crisp and bright.

6 Rub back any painted metal decoration, such as this brass edging, with sandpaper to reveal just a touch of shiny metal. Apply a final coat of clear wax all over with a clean, dry cloth.

painted lamp bases

Finding interesting lamp bases can be something of a challenge. I really liked the shape of these two that I found in a secondhand store in France. The larger base is made of porcelain, elaborately decorated and colored, while the smaller one is plainer and made from marble.

Porcelain is very shiny and non-absorbent, which means that any paint covering will take quite a long time to dry. Marble, like onyx, on the other hand, is quite absorbent, so takes the paint very well and dries more quickly. I chose to paint both lamp bases in neutral colors—the porcelain in French Linen, and the marble in Coco—so that nothing would detract from their shape.

YOU WILL NEED

- French Linen paint, for the porcelain lamp base
- Coco paint, for the marble lamp base
- Large, oval brush
- Clear wax
- 1in (2.5cm) brush, to apply the wax (optional)
- Clean, dry, lint-free cloths

Tip: My paint, Chalk Paint®, can be applied to more or less any surface, including ceramic, pottery, and plastic.

1 Cover the porcelain with French Linen paint, using the large, oval brush. As the porcelain is smooth and shiny, be careful not to overbrush because this will cause the paint to come off the raised areas. Alternatively, you could make this a feature of your design, in which case you need to apply a bit more pressure with the brush. Paint the marble lamp base with Coco paint. Put both bases to one side until the paint is completely dry and hard. This will take about a day for the porcelain base but less time for the marble base.

OPPOSITE *The gaudy colored porcelain lamp base has been transformed into a piece that looks carved from stone. Painted in French Linen, it harmonizes with the other neutrals here—the wash of Country Grey over French Linen on the side table, and French Linen with Aubusson Blue on the picture frame.*

2 Cover the porcelain base gently with clear wax, using the 1in (2.5cm) brush. I could have pressed more firmly so that some of the porcelain would come through on the raised area but I decided against it because I wanted the look to be as simple as possible. Gently remove any excess wax with a clean, dry cloth. Wax the marble base in the same way.

boho chic

Probably the most inspiring group of artists for me is the Bloomsbury Group. They painted the furniture and walls of Charleston Farmhouse (their base in Sussex, in the south of England) in a free and colorful way and it has remained one of the most influential types of decoration for me since I began painting interiors over 30 years ago.

Boho chic is a style of interiors that takes its inspiration from a less formal and a more relaxed way of living. The word boho comes from "bohemian," usually used to describe an artist who has an unconventional life although when applied to interiors it means a slightly off-beat, unconventional design style and because of this, by definition, it's difficult to pin down.

Some people call it "hippy chic" and use ethnic colors inspired by India and Morocco and use it with floaty fabrics. Others are inspired by artists' work and the studio lifestyle, pulling in color combinations and design motifs from a particular artist and a random collection of inspiring objects. Everyone's interpretation could be a little different and there certainly is an overlap with modern and retro decoration as well as all the other styles. Probably the most important element of Boho Chic is that it challenges conventional thinking and deconstructs history. For me, Boho Chic begins in Paris at around the turn of the 19th century when Paris was daring and radical and the artist lifestyle began to establish itself. Picasso, Matisse, and many other artists were inspired by African art as well as traditional elements, too, but in a loose way.

Color combinations in Boho Chic tend to be less expected, and more secondary and tertiary colors are used together—various greens, oranges, and lilacs, with turquoise, aquamarine, pinks, and quite a lot of black to make the colors pop out. Barcelona Orange, Emile, Provence, Florence, and Antibes Green,with pinks such as Henrietta and Antoinette, are essential to the boho look.

painted and gilded bed

I started with the French Napoleonic bed in this room, painting it in Antibes Green, then gilding the central classical laurel leaves and shield on the bedhead. The bed now has an outrageous pomposity about it, although the overall look of the room is not at all ostentatious—the mud walls are painted in Old White (see page 126) and the side table in Antibes Green mixed with Louis Blue (see page 62). On the right is a Provençal chair still with its original paint. As I complete the decoration of the room, more colors will be added but the focus will remain on the bedhead.

YOU WILL NEED

- Antibes Green paint
- Round bristle brush, no. 8 or 12
- Water-based gold size
- Book of brass leaf
- Small soft-haired brush, to apply the size
- Firm, dry brush, to push down the brass leaf
- Large brush, to apply the wax
- Clear wax
- Dark wax
- Plenty of clean, dry lint-free cloths, to rub the wax on and off and to polish

1 Let the paint "dry out" a little by keeping the lid off the can for a day or two before you start work—this will thicken the paint slightly, resulting in a better texture. Apply the paint over the entire bed with the round bristle brush, making the brush marks obvious by working in many different directions. Stab the paint into the carved areas to ensure all the detailing is covered.

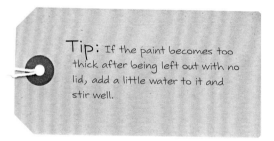

Tip: If the paint becomes too thick after being left out with no lid, add a little water to it and stir well.

2 A second coat of paint may be necessary if the wood is very shiny or has been waxed recently. Make sure the first coat is dry before applying the second. Continue to make the brush marks obvious and stab the paint into the carved areas. Allow to dry thoroughly.

3 When the paint is completely dry, use a small soft-haired brush to apply a layer of gold size over the leaves and shield where you want to have the brass leaf. Wait a few minutes before applying a second coat of size, to make certain that the area is thoroughly covered. Allow the size to go completely clear, when it will be sticky.

4 Lay a sheet of brass leaf—it doesn't matter which side faces up— over a section of the carving. Starting at the highest point, dab down with a firm brush to press the leaf into place. Lay the leaf as flat as you can, making sure it has stuck to the gold size. Continue in this way with more sheets of leaf until you have covered the entire carving.

5 To achieve good coverage and to make the "gold" appear solid, apply another layer of size and put a second layer of leaf on top of the first, as above.

6 Dab the leaf down firmly into all the crevices and curves of the carving with the brush, to make sure it is properly stuck. Sweep away the excess leaf with the brush.

7 Wipe the gilded areas with a thin layer of clear wax using the brush. Make sure that the wax covers every part of the carving. Wipe away any excess with a clean, dry cloth.

8 Cover the carving with a layer of dark wax, stabbing with the brush so that it reaches all the crevices.

ABOVE *I painted Antibes Green thickly and unevenly over the entire bed and then applied a dark wax to bring out the texture of the wood. I deliberately kept the top of the panel lighter—it looked too heavy with the dark wax on top, and the gold looked lighter and brighter when I wiped the wax off. Gilding the magnificent classical shield with laurel leaves makes the bedhead the focus of the room.*

9 Spread the wax more thinly with a cloth and remove any excess. Use a dry brush, if necessary, to remove any build-up of dark wax in the crevices.

10 If you want to remove any of the leaf for a more distressed effect, wipe over the leaves and shield once more with clear wax, pressing a little harder.

Tip: Always apply clear wax before dark wax. Without the layer of clear wax, the dark wax will stain the paint, which will make it impossible to revert to the original color of the wood.

11 Wax the rest of the bed, first with clear wax, followed by dark wax, as above. Work on a small area at a time so that the clear wax doesn't dry before the next step. If the dark wax is too dark, you can remove it with some clear wax until you achieve exactly the look you are after.

mixing a color

Antibes Green is a strong color with a lot of impact so the side table needed to be softer, although another green, a neutral, or white would not enhance the green. On the other side of the room I plan to have a chest of drawers painted in Emile (a strong lilac), but the piece next to the bed needed to pick up on the bed color. Boho chic combos tend to be colorful, but in the same tonal area and not clashing. I liked the idea of blue and green together and tried Duck Egg Blue, but this looked too flat and gray so I used Antibes Green as the base coat and added Louis Blue to it to soften it. Antibes Green was used to paint the inside of the drawer.

YOU WILL NEED

- Antibes Green paint
- Louis Blue paint
- Oval brush
- Clear wax
- 2 small bristle brushes, to apply and spread the wax
- Clean, dry, lint-free cloth

1 I wanted a color for the bedside table that would not detract from the magnificence of the bed. A quiet color was called for. I first tried Duck Egg Blue but this looked too gray in comparison to the liveliness of Antibes Green.

2 I then tried Louis Blue. Although too blue on its own, it was perfect when mixed half and half with Antibes Green.

3 For the bedside table I needed about a cup of each color, which I judged by pouring directly from the can into a roller tray and mixing well.

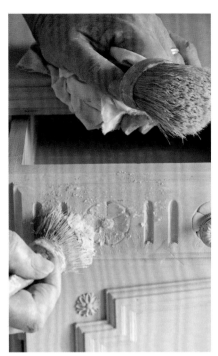

4 This bedside table had a marble top, which I also wanted to paint. Using the oval bristle brush, apply the paint in all directions in a series of long and short strokes. You may need to return to cover small areas that you have missed. Let the top dry.

5 Remove the drawer, and paint the rest of the table. Make certain that you reach the more inaccessible places by stabbing the paint into the wood. Paint the outside of the drawer separately.

6 After the paint has dried—this should take about 30 minutes—apply clear wax all over the table with the wax brush. Again, stab with the brush to make sure all the detailing is covered.

7 Wipe over the wax with a dry bristle brush, to spread the wax out even more thinly and ensure that it is fully absorbed into the paint. Use a stabbing motion around the carving. Finally, wipe over the entire table with a dry cloth so the paint is completely covered in wax but does not look greasy. As I wanted this piece to look fairly matte, I didn't polish it.

RIGHT *I painted the inside of the bedside table drawer with Antibes Green to link in with the bed, although I did toy with the idea of a lilac or purple, such as Emile.*

painted fabric chair

I found a perfectly shaped Louis XV-style armchair in a French market, but the seat and back were upholstered in an old-fashioned, dirty yellow, mock velvet. Rather than having the chair re-covered, as I was in a hurry to use it, I simply got out my paintbrush and set to work. Painted fabric, even if it has a pile, is perfectly comfortable and does not leave you covered in paint, as you might think!

Painting the wood was easy enough but this was the first time I had ever tried to paint fabric that had a pile, so it was all down to trial and error. The fabric needed to be painted in such a way that the pile didn't disappear or get clogged with paint, making it hard and crusty. Adding the right amount of water to the paint was crucial, so that it covered the fabric and was absorbed. At my first attempt, I applied the paint too thickly in places but it was not until it had dried that I was aware of how hard and thick it had made the fabric surface.

I chose Paloma, a gray color made by mixing yellow and purple together with white, to paint both the fabric and the wood. Purple and yellow are complementary colors, and painting Paloma over the yellow mock velvet resulted in a harmonious blend.

ABOVE *The whole chair is painted in Paloma, with just a little Old White added to the arms and around the back. Only the woodwork was waxed. The paint on the upholstery studs was wiped and softly sanded to reveal a touch of gold. Here and there on the fabric, I painted the Paloma on a little thicker for added interest. The cushion is made from my Normandie toile fabric, in a pale lilac.*

ABOVE *An alternative to using Paloma for this project is to mix Emile, a warm soft eggplant (aubergine) color, and Arles, a rich yellow. This creates a very dark gray, which you can then tweak according to how much of each color you use. Adding a little Old White to the mix gives a color close to Paloma, shown here on its own to the right.*

Tip: To make certain of the consistency of the paint is a question of trial and error. Test a small patch on the back of the chair first before painting the entire thing.

YOU WILL NEED

- Paloma paint
- Old White paint
- Large oval brush, for painting the fabric
- Paint roller tray
- Medium oval brush, for painting the wood
- Clear wax, for the wood
- Brush and/or clean, dry, lint-free cloth, to apply the wax
- Fine sandpaper

1 Paint the wood with Paloma paint using the oval brush. The paint should be of standard consistency, so that it flows on smoothly and easily. Let the paint dry. (I added the Old White line once the chair was finished as I felt it needed something more.)

2 To cover the fabric, dilute the Paloma paint with water so that it is liquid enough to be absorbed. I mixed mine in a roller tray. The paint needs to soak into the "top" of the chair, rather than all the way through—what you are trying to avoid is thick paint that clogs up the pile

and feels hard and crusty on drying. If you think the paint might still be too thick, add some more water and use a scrubbing motion with the paintbrush to spread the paint around. Let the paint dry—it took a few summer days for the fabric on my chair to dry out thoroughly.

3 Use a brush or clean, dry cloth to apply clear wax thinly and evenly over the woodwork. Wipe off any excess with a cloth, and wipe the upholstery studs. Sand them gently to reveal the gold color underneath.

copper leaf bath

This little corner of my Normandy bedroom is a boho-chic country haven. I had hankered after a freestanding copper bath for years—they are so sumptuous yet earthy-looking. One way of acquiring one was to cover the outside of my enamel roll-top bath in copper leaf.

Copper is a very warm and rich, gingery red color and, as it's a shiny metal, emits light. To soften its appearance, something cool and deep was needed underneath it, to show through. Florence—a coppery green paint, similar to the color of verdigris—was perfect. I could have used a bright blue instead, such as Greek Blue or Aubusson Blue or a mix of the two, but decided against it because the room was predominantly blue and I didn't want everything the same.

The bath has been mounted on black slate, and around the edge of it I put a wooden border, painted in a coat of thinned-out Graphite. I then covered it with clear wax so the wood shows through a little, to work with the wash on the floor. The planks of rough wood on the wall behind the bath have been colorwashed in a mix of Duck Egg Blue and Florence, using a damp sponge in the same way that I painted the floor on page 106. The wonderful contrast of the shiny copper next to the matte of the wood and the floors is very soothing and pleasing. Napoleon, in an old print on the wall, surveys the scene.

WHAT YOU WILL NEED
- Florence paint
- Medium oval brush
- Water-based gold size
- Flat synthetic brush, to apply the gold size
- Sheets of copper leaf
- Talcum powder (optional)
- Dry, firm but soft-haired brush, to push down the copper leaf
- Clear wax
- Soft, clean, dry, lint-free cloth, to apply the wax

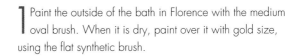

1 Paint the outside of the bath in Florence with the medium oval brush. When it is dry, paint over it with gold size, using the flat synthetic brush.

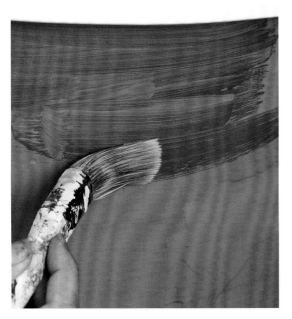

2 While the size is becoming clear, take a sheet of copper leaf and lightly crumple it in your hands. If you find the leaf sticks to your hands, put a light covering of talcum powder on them. Gently flatten out the leaf.

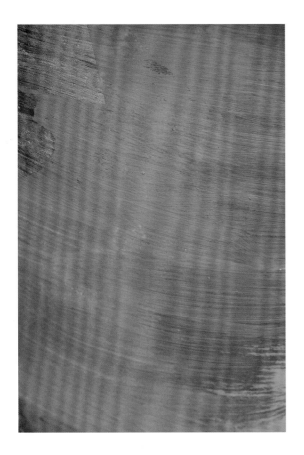

LEFT *Size starts out as white, quickly turns to a rather luminescent ultraviolet color for a minute or so, then becomes clear. At this point, it is ready to be used, although it will actually remain sticky for several weeks or more. I normally apply the size all at once to the area I am working on. When choosing colors, bear in mind that the size makes the paint darken.*

3 Lay the flattened sheet of leaf on the sticky size—don't do this until the size is completely clear with no white areas. I like to lay the leaf on with one hand and hold the firm brush in the other and use it to position the leaf.

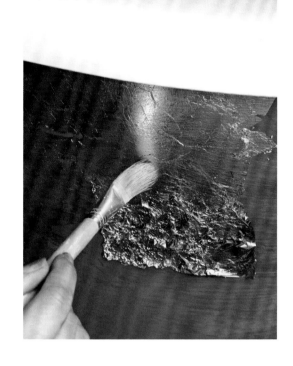

4 Brush the leaf all over firmly. The folds in the leaf will make small cracks and gaps so the green paint underneath will show through. The finish will probably look quite messy at this point. Repeat steps 2–4 with the remaining sheets of copper leaf.

Tip: You might consider leaving the copper leaf to darken and tarnish slightly before applying the wax. Once the wax is applied, the air can't get to the leaf anymore, so the tarnishing process is arrested.

5 Once you have applied the copper leaf all over the side of the bath, use a soft cloth to coat it with clear wax. This will remove any excess gold leaf and flatten everything out, giving a smooth finish. If you want to see more of the green underneath, rub a little harder so that some of the copper leaf is removed.

painted chandelier

The central room in the house has been decorated in a cool, restrained, and classical Swedish style, which I love. However, I wanted to add a little bit of color and embellishment, to make a connection to my stenciled walls, which are quite lively. I decided to do this by painting the rather shiny brass chandelier.

The chandelier needed to be softer and matte, rather than shiny, to suit the room. I first tried painting it in Scandinavian Pink and Country Grey but that was just too conservative. Knowing that Scandinavia has an interesting craft tradition with a playful element to it, I felt justified in approaching the decoration in a more bohemian way but still using a traditional Swedish color palette. First, I experimented with dots but they didn't look right, and I ended up painting the chandelier with stripes and wobbly lines, using small artists' paintbrushes.

YOU WILL NEED

- A selection of paints (I used Duck Egg Blue, Château Grey, Scandinavian Pink, Arles, Greek Blue, Provence, Louis Blue, Burgundy, Old White, Country Grey, Primer Red, Aubusson Blue)
- No. 8 bristle brush, for main part of the chandelier
- No. 4 and 6 artists' brushes, for detailing

LEFT *For this project, I put together a collection of colors that were all inspired by Scandinavia: Scandinavian Pink, Primer Red, Arles, and Burgundy, with the cooler shades of Old White, Château Grey, and Provence. I ended up using very little Arles and adding Louis Blue, Greek Blue, and Country Grey to the combinations, so the colors are all very harmonious.*

1 Highlight the shapes of the light fitting by picking out various elements in colors that work with the rest of the room. I painted around the edges of the "saucer" fittings in Louis Blue, but then introduced a touch of boho chic by painting the candle-shaped sleeves in Burgundy.

2 Paint the entire ball of the chandelier in Duck Egg Blue. When dry, paint continuous lines, some thicker than others, around the ball in other shades of blue and white over the top, using the artists' brushes. Do this with a light, almost "nervous" touch, just taking your brush off the surface when you need to reposition your hand. Vary the distance between the lines for added interest. Paint the part of the fitting above the ball in a solid Aubusson Blue.

3 Using similar colors, paint the stem of the light fitting in lines as well. Paint the long pipelines in Château Grey and Duck Egg Blue, dipping the brush in the colors alternately to give a varied look. These colors are very similar in tone and so blur together very well.

printed cabinet

A certain freedom of design is possible with printing because you don't have to be so concerned with painting. For your patterns to work, keep in mind the idea of randomness, chance, the loose and the unexpected, and a sense of playfulness. At first, it's probably best not to work with too many colors and patterns, and wait until you have a clear idea about what you want to do, rather than forcing it. Use a sketchbook to develop your ideas and create different patterns and borders for the various parts of the piece of furniture, such as the drawer front, moldings, and base of this cabinet.

Before doing any printing, I painted this cabinet all over in Old White with a medium oval brush and left it to dry. I then painted a 3in (8cm) border around the top of the cabinet in Versailles.

YOU WILL NEED
- Coco paint
- Burgundy paint
- Greek Blue paint
- Versailles paint
- Old White paint
- Reusable adhesive, such as Blu-Tack
- Medium, flat brush
- Small, flat brush
- Toilet-tissue tube
- Eraser
- Craft knife
- Polystyrene packing
- Clear wax
- 1in (2.5cm) flat brush, for applying the wax
- Clean, dry, lint-free cloth

ABOVE *On a background of Coco, a warm gray-brown, a pattern of overlapping circles in Old White has been created on the drawer with the end of a toilet-tissue tube. Similarly, on the molding above, a Greek Blue wash over the Coco has been decorated with semicircles in Burgundy.*

ABOVE *So many things can be used to make prints, and half the fun of printing is searching out interesting implements. Here, I have used reusable adhesive such as Blu-Tack, a cork, bottle lids, an eraser, a toilet-tissue tube, and polystyrene.*

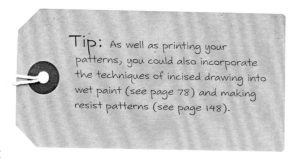

Tip: As well as printing your patterns, you could also incorporate the techniques of incised drawing into wet paint (see page 78) and making resist patterns (see page 148).

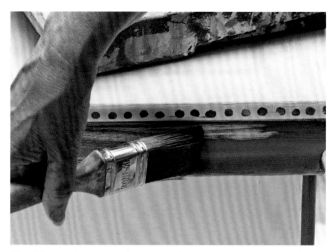

1 Break off some reusable adhesive, such as Blu-Tack, roll it up, then dip one end into the Coco paint. Make little spots of Coco, evenly spaced, along the molding edge. Although varied in size and a little erratic in shape, there is a certain pleasing consistency about these spots.

2 The background to any pattern is important, and it is easier to design on a color than on white. Add enough water to the Coco to create a watery wash. Using the medium, flat brush, paint this all over the front and sides of the cabinet, including the next tier of molding but excluding the base of the cabinet. Paint the base in Burgundy.

3 Add enough water to the Greek Blue to create a watery wash. When the Coco is almost dry, brush the wash roughly over the next tier of molding. Let it dry.

4 Using the small, flat brush, paint halfway around the edge of one end of the toilet-tissue tube with Burgundy. This will give you a semicircle shape with which to print.

5 Dab the painted end of the tube along the molding edge underneath the spots of Coco. Press down firmly, taking care not to move the tube as you do so. Repaint the end of the tube as necessary.

6 Cut a sliver off the eraser with the craft knife, to give you a sharp edge. Dip this into the Greek Blue paint, then make a short but solid blue line under each Burgundy arch.

7 Mix a dilute wash of Versailles (one part paint to four parts water) and paint a strip around the edge of the table top. Mine was 2in (5cm) wide, but this will vary according to the size of the table top. Press the polystyrene rectangle into the wet paint to make an imprint. Repeat this, wiping the excess wet paint from the polystyrene.

Tip: Polystyrene from packaging is a great material for making patterns. It is easy to cut with a craft knife, and fashion into simple squares and rectangles as well as more fanciful shapes.

8 Paint all the way around the edge of the other end of the toilet-tissue tube with Old White. Make a pattern of overlapping circles on the drawer front. Press down firmly, taking care not to move the tube as you do so. Repaint the end of the tube as necessary.

9 Brush over the entire cabinet with clear wax, wiping away any excess with a clean, dry cloth as you go.

RIGHT *I also used printing to decorate a picture frame. The blue spotty sky was created out of bubble wrap; the houses from an eraser cut into various shapes; and the brown stripy background from a cotton bud dipped into a mix of complementary Primer Red and Antibes Green.*

incised painted cabinet

I love drawing into wet paint with the end of a paintbrush. It's all very liberating and, of course, good fun, because if you make a mistake while the paint is still wet, you can simply remove it by painting it out.

I wanted to decorate the door panels of this cabinet with something quite light-hearted, uncomplicated, and not too derivative. Stick men immediately came to mind because everyone can draw them. My stick man turned into a rather comic character, and one that I've become rather fond of. I decided to use Old White and Graphite, to create a striking contrast.

Before you draw into wet paint, it's important to practice on paper beforehand so that your design isn't tentative. I started off by imagining and marking out in my head where all the coordinates of the drawing would be.

YOU WILL NEED

● Graphite paint
● Old White paint
● Paper and pencil
● Medium oval brush
● End of a small wooden paintbrush or similar
● Small, flat brush
● Clear wax
● Small, flat wax brush
● Clean, dry, lint-free cloth

LEFT *The little cabinet hangs on a Paris Grey wall, with Provence painted behind the doors. Traditional French cider cups lined up on the shelf make a delightful contrast.*

1 Start off by drawing lots of stick men on paper, varying the proportions of the body, head, and legs, and also the positions of the arms and legs. Getting the size of the drawing on the panels is important, too. I wanted my design to have as much impact as possible, so I drew it as large as it could be, with a bit of space around it.

2 Using the medium oval brush, paint the entire cabinet, excluding the panels, with Graphite covering over the previous color. Then brush on Old White in the panels. Allow the paint to dry thoroughly, so it is firm when you begin to draw into it.

3 Paint a rough-edged background in Graphite on the panel—do this thinly with paint that is a little on the dry side. Immediately, while the paint is still wet, start to draw.

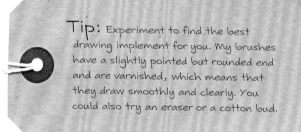

Tip: Experiment to find the best drawing implement for you. My brushes have a slightly pointed but rounded end and are varnished, which means that they draw smoothly and clearly. You could also try an eraser or a cotton bud.

4 Dip the wooden end of the small paintbrush into the Graphite, then press firmly into the Old White as you draw. If you make a mistake, just paint over the area and start again while the paint is still wet. Draw relatively slowly and carefully but firmly and decisively.

5 Paint around the edges of the cabinet in Old White using the small, flat brush, to add contrast.

6 With the end of the small paintbrush, draw lines into the Old White so that you can see the Graphite underneath. I have drawn these freely so they have a playful look about them.

7 Load the flat brush with Old White and gently wipe it along the bottom edge of the cabinet, to leave an uneven hand-painted line. Reload the brush as needed.

8 Once all the paint is dry, apply a coat of clear wax over the entire cabinet with the wax brush, then polish it lightly with the cloth, to give a nice matte finish.

decoupage sideboard

This sideboard, or buffet, as it is known in France, was given to me by my neighbor in Normandy, Marie Gaillard. (I have also used her monogrammed linen for the Dyeing Fabric with Paint project on pages 36–39.) I painted and decorated the sideboard many years ago for the house, and it can be seen in an earlier book of mine called *Annie Sloan's Decoupage*. Since then, I have had a bit more fun with it. I used some amusing and rather brightly colored wrapping paper with vintage luggage labels on it to decorate it. For the two central panels, I folded the paper in half and cut out a shape resembling a plant in a pot. The inspiration for this project came from traditional Eastern European paper cutting, which is very intricate; making paper dolly chains, which I did as a child; and also patchwork.

YOU WILL NEED

● Large sheet of plain paper or wrapping paper, to fit the sideboard panel

● Sharp scissors

● Pencil

● All-in-one Annie Sloan decoupage glue and varnish

● 1in (2.5cm) flat brush

● Coarse sandpaper

● Clear wax

● 1in (2.5cm) brush, to apply the wax

● Clean, dry, lint-free cloth

1 Cut the paper so that it fits into the panel. Fold the paper in half.

2 Draw one half of the plant pot at the folded edge of the paper, and the central stalk of the plant, with branches and a few big leaves coming off it. Make sure the stalk and the branches are not too thin, and that there are no gaps within the design.

3 Carefully cut out the design in one connected piece.

Tip: If using a wrapping paper for your decoupage, choose a densely patterned design or an extremely plain one, to contrast with the color of the furniture underneath.

LEFT *I originally painted the entire sideboard with Aubusson Blue over Barcelona Orange, sanding a little before finally varnishing. The decoupage flowerpots were cut out from wrapping paper depicting vintage luggage labels, while the four red strips are done in plain red paper. Since then, I have added more Barcelona Orange, which brings out the colors of the central panels and painted the drawers in Olive over Barcelona Orange. I varnished the papered areas with an all-in-one decoupage medium, before lightly rubbing with coarse sandpaper for a delicate, worn effect. I then covered the decoupage with a coat of clear wax, to soften the look.*

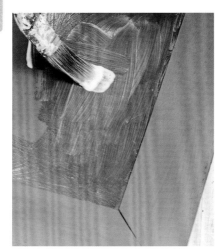

4 Apply the decoupage medium fairly generously over the entire panel, so that it stays wet.

5 Take the paper and, starting at the top, very carefully position it on the panel, making certain that it goes on straight. Brush over the paper as you go with more decoupage medium to make certain the paper is sticking well and also to protect it.

6 When the decoupage medium is dry, rub over the paper lightly with coarse sandpaper, to give a slightly worn effect. Use the wax brush to apply a coat of clear wax over the entire panel, removing any excess with a clean, dry cloth.

swedish style

Ever since I began decorative painting over 30 years ago, I have been aware of the immense legacy of traditional Swedish painted interiors. I was so inspired by the custom of itinerant painters who went from one farmhouse to the next, decorating the walls and furniture in traditional scenes and patterns. (Early Swedish settlers took the same tradition to the US, too.) The painters used a palette of indigenous earth-greens, a deep brown-red called Falu Red—the ubiquitous red-ocher found everywhere in Scandinavia that inspired me to make my Scandinavian Pink—plus a warm yellow ocher, and also whites.

In the 18th century, the Swedish aristocracy looked to France for elegance and grandeur, and set out to re-create the French style in their palaces. Blessed with an abundance of wood from their pine forests, and with the itinerant painting tradition, they painted just about everything, from walls to floors and furniture, imitating the moldings and carvings that they so admired in the French palaces. This combination of French style and Swedish materials and craftsmen led to an exquisite look that has motivated a great deal of painted work in recent years.

The central room in my house is the grandest, as the ceiling is quite high and the double windows are a good size. We installed a brand new pine staircase leading to new bedrooms upstairs, which needed to be painted. This is where the Swedish theme began. The staircase seemed to demand to be painted in whites and grays, while the wall alongside called for painted panels. I had stenciled the walls many years previously and I was unhappy about painting them out when Christopher Drake, our photographer, commented on how perfectly Swedish they were. He had photographed many old Swedish interiors, and knew what he was talking about, so the walls stayed. The room is basically cool blues and whites with Château Grey and the warmer colors of Primer Red and Scandinavian Pink. Other warm colors appear in the wall stenciling.

The Swedish palette is basically the same as the French palette but with a greater emphasis on Aubusson Blue, Old White, and Paris Grey, and could also include Château Grey, Scandinavian Pink, Arles, and Primer Red.

painted panel wall

The staircase (see page 90) that we installed to reach the new rooms we had created upstairs meant that the stenciled wall had to be re-plastered, obliterating my original design. This led me to look at the wall in a fresh way. I felt it needed a calm and quiet design that would work harmoniously with the staircase and the rest of the old stenciling in the room. I have long been a fan of 18th-century Swedish, where painted lines—just one or two of various thicknesses, often in blues, grays, or the traditional earthy Swedish pink—were used on walls to indicate panels.

Painting lines on walls is difficult and requires a lot of practice, so I have devised a method that can allow you to be less precise. A roughly textured wall, rather than a perfectly smooth one, gives the best results. To make a smooth wall rough, paint it first with a bristle brush in different directions, allowing the paint to be uneven with brush marks, or plaster it with an uneven finish.

The brushes I used for this project are specialist fresco brushes, with a long pointy tip designed for painting lines. They are not essential for this project but you do need to use fine, long-haired brushes with soft but strong bristles. The brush also has to be able to hold a lot of paint so you can pull it along without having to reload. I used brushes of two different widths to create the lines of different thicknesses.

LEFT AND RIGHT *The room originally had a dado rail but all that remains now is part of the original wiring system at the same height. I decided to treat the area beneath the wiring like a dado, using paint to delineate it. Traditionally, the dado is painted in a darker color than the area above the rail—I chose Country Grey. I then painted thin blue lines to represent the panels.*

YOU WILL NEED

- Old White paint
- Country Grey paint
- Aubusson Blue paint
- Pencil
- Long, straight piece of molding
- No. 2 flat brush, to paint the Old White and Country Grey
- Round-sided molding, to act as a guide
- Oval brushes, to paint the Old White
- 2 fine brushes of different widths, to paint the lines
- Fine sandpaper
- Clear wax
- Clean, dry, lint-free cloth, to rub the wax on and off

ABOVE *I worked out beforehand where the panels should be on the stairway by doing a rough drawing and making some notes about the colors. I decided on using Old White in the center panels; Country Grey, a warm soft pale brown-gray on the outer areas; and Aubusson Blue lightened with Old White for the lines. The lines around the center panels were painted more thickly than those of the outer frame.*

1 Paint the entire wall in Old White with a flat brush. Roughly work out the size and shape of the panels by eye and, with a pencil, lightly mark where you think they will go on the wall. When you have finally decided on the size of each panel, mark them out on the wall using a long straight piece of molding as a guide. Paint the outside area between the panels in Country Grey using a flat brush to work up to the pencil lines.

2 Lighten the Aubusson Blue by mixing it with Old White (roughly two-thirds blue to one-third white, but the quantity of white depends how light you wish the blue to be—a larger room can take a more distinct difference between the two tones). Hold the molding against a pencil line, to act as a guide—this will allow a loaded brush to glide along it without paint seeping underneath. Load the thinner fine brush with paint. As you paint the lines, use your little finger as a guide, letting it slide along the side of the wood as you paint, keeping your finger and wrist firm so the brush stays steady and straight. This will allow paint to flow from the brush evenly and at the same rate. Paint thicker lines in the same way, using the thicker brush.

Tip: Before painting the lines, have a dry run first to apply the paint evenly. You may need to hold your body in a certain position to do so.

3 When the paint lines are dry, rub them gently with fine sandpaper, particularly where they are too thick or wobbly, to let the texture of the wall come through. Lightly wax the wall, taking care not to polish it so that it remains matte and not shiny.

textured staircase

The new pine staircase in my Swedish-inspired room had little character, which was in stark contrast to the rest of the house. It needed texture and an aged appearance in order to fit in. I have long admired the Swedish style of using whites and grays on pine, and as the walls in this room are where all the action is, I decided that sanding the edges of the steps and applying quiet washes of Old White and Paris Grey would give just the right look.

I painted and lacquered the stairs first (see caption, below). Although the photographs and instructions overleaf are for the bannisters, the stairs were painted using the same technique. The staircase now looks as if it has always belonged in the house.

YOU WILL NEED
- Old White paint
- Paris Grey paint
- Clear shellac (knotting solution)
- Plenty of clean, dry, lint-free cloths
- No. 8 or 12 oval brush
- Sponge
- 2–3in (5–8cm) flat brush
- Coarse, medium, and fine sandpaper
- Matte lacquer
- 3in (8cm) brush, for applying the lacquer

LEFT *Before painting, I rubbed the edges of each step with coarse sandpaper to give the appearance of scuffing from many years of footfall. To reinforce this aged appearance after painting and to make the stairs look as natural as possible, we used them for several weeks before applying a protective coat of matte lacquer. I could have waxed the stairs instead, for a softer look, but this would require more upkeep. A compromise would be to lacquer the stairs but wax the bannisters.*

1 Add a squirt of water to the Paris Grey paint, so it is runny but not translucent. Apply one coat of paint to the bannisters with an oval brush in every direction, so that there will be a few brush marks in the dried paint, creating texture.

2 With a damp sponge, wipe off areas here and there to suggest gentle wearing over time. Have a clean, dry cloth ready to wipe off any excess paint and water so you can see the effect you have created.

3 Add a squirt of water to the Old White paint, if necessary. To make the bannisters look as if they have been worn away in places, apply a coat of paint with a flat brush, working the paint lightly here and there to give a dragged effect.

4 After about 10 minutes, when the paint seems touch-dry, wipe away the Old White in places with a damp sponge, to reveal the texture of the brushwork.

5 Rub the bannisters gently here and there with medium and fine sandpaper to suggest the paint has worn away to the wood. When all the paint is dry, cover the bannisters with a protective coat of matte lacquer.

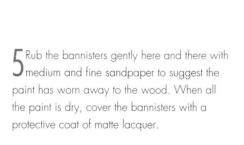

Tip: Before you start, check for knots in the new wood. If there are quite a few, you will need to apply clear shellac (knotting solution), to prevent the sap in the knots bleeding though the paint— this can happen for up to a year after painting— leaving a yellowish-orange stain. Dab the liquid onto a cloth and wipe over the knot. It will dry almost immediately.

stenciled wall

Many years ago when we first lived in our house in Normandy, I stenciled the walls in the room that I now grandly call the study. I made a big stencil out of Manila paper and, as I only had the one, I had to use it until it fell apart, with several broken stencil bridges. I stenciled randomly, using several colors one on top of another, mixing them as I went on in a roller tray with a sponge roller.

Years later, returning to the work I did then, I realized that some walls needed refreshing because of building work that had since taken place. Some of the stencils I left as they were, while I gave others a wash of Old White applied with a sponge, to tone them down. Other parts of the wall were very patchy or rather worn, as they had been covered by furniture, so I found a similar damask-style stencil and tried to re-create the original design.

YOU WILL NEED

- 4 or more paint colors that work well together
- Old White paint
- 2 roller trays
- 2 sponge rollers
- Damask pattern stencil
- Large flat brush
- Sponge

LEFT *Before you start stenciling, arrange all your materials. The paints I used were Paris Grey, Château Grey, Duck Egg Blue, Arles, Scandinavian Pink, Old Violet, and Primer Red.*

1 Pour two colors into a roller tray. Roll the sponge roller into the paint so half of it is covered in one color, and the other half in the second color. Don't soak the sponge too much, as a small amount of paint goes a long way.

RIGHT *This is the stenciling I did many years ago, using my own paints. My inspiration had come from the simple stencil designs on the walls of those American farmhouses lived in by early Swedish settlers, who decorated their homes using this traditional painting style and technique. With my stenciling, I had intended to reflect the passing of time, with some of the stencils looking as if they had faded and some as if they had been replaced.*

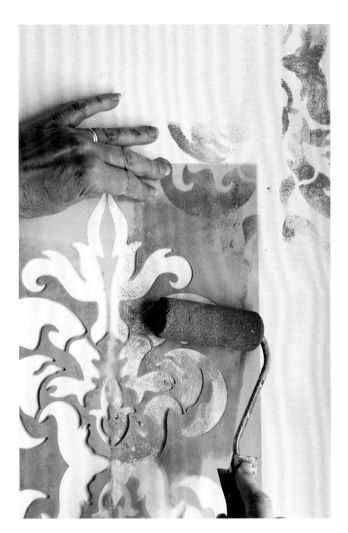

2 Place the stencil on the wall with one hand and, with the other, gently roll the roller on random parts of the stencil. Move the stencil to another part of the wall and do the same thing but using another part of the design. When you replenish the paint, don't worry about getting the mix exactly the same—the random mix is what gives this stenciling its charm.

3 Pour two different colors into another tray. Roll the second sponge roller in the tray, as above. Place the stencil on the wall again and apply the color. Trust your gut feeling to make the design more overlapped and denser in places and lighter in others. Don't get too absorbed in the detail but think about the wall as a whole.

4 When you have finished the wall, either leave it as it is or give it a wash of Old White paint, to knock the design back. Wet a large brush, dip it into the paint, and apply lightly to a workable area of about 20sq in (50sq cm).

5 With a lightly damp sponge, immediately wipe over the surface lightly so that the Old White creates a veil of translucent white over the stencil design. If any parts of the stencil stand out too much, lighten them with an extra splotch of Old White. Move on rapidly to the next area. Add a little more water to the sponge or more paint to lighten or whiten as you work. If the paint is too opaque, just wipe it with the damp sponge with a little more force.

dry-painted armoire

Old pieces of furniture that have been left out in sheds or backyards so the varnish has all but disappeared, giving a chalky and bleached look, are very to difficult to come by. With that in mind, I decided to re-create this beautiful effect on a very shiny brown armoire by painting it, first with Graphite, followed by Old White. I used Scandinavian Pink for the insides, including the backs of the doors and inside the drawers. This warm shade contrasts well with the Old White and picks up on the colors in the wall stencils (see page 94).

ABOVE *I painted directly over the key escutcheon, then wiped a little paint off with a dry cloth, to reveal just a shimmer of the original brass.*

YOU WILL NEED

- Graphite paint
- Old White paint
- No. 8 or 12 oval bristle brush
- Clear wax
- Large brush, to apply the wax
- Clean, dry, lint-free cloth

1 Paint the entire armoire in Graphite, moving the brush in every direction, to create a little bit of texture.

LEFT *When painted over the Graphite, the Old White on the armoire takes on a grayish tinge, which is picked up by the floor and staircase painted in Paris Grey. The other main colors in the room are Château Grey, Country Grey, Scandinavian Pink, and Aubusson Blue.*

2 By the time you have finished painting the base color on a large piece of furniture like this armoire, the paint where you started will be dry. Dip the end of a dry brush in the Old White paint and wipe over, using the tip of the brush at first, then a scrubbing motion over the surface.

3 Working quickly, make certain that the paint is brushed out really well so there are no obvious brush marks. Use a stabbing motion to push the paint into any crevices.

Tip: The wax should be wet enough to remove with a cloth but not so wet that it all comes off in one wipe. After waxing, wash brushes in soap and warm water to restore the shape.

4 The Old White will become a little gray in places, and the paint will sometimes wipe off completely, revealing the brown varnished wood underneath, but this all adds to the character of the piece. Add a little bit of paint at a time rather than loading the brush up.

5 Apply a layer of clear wax with the 2in (5cm) brush. Work on a small area at a time so that the wax doesn't dry before you wipe off the excess with a dry cloth, leaving a fine layer of wax.

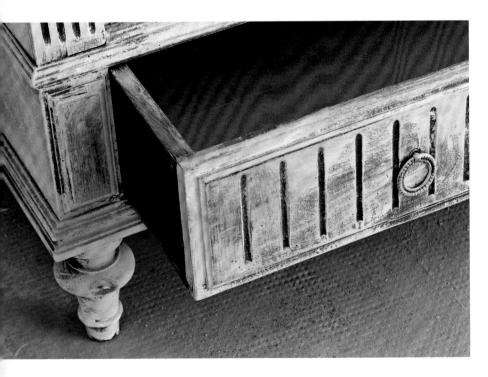

LEFT *Scandinavian Pink, used on the insides of the drawers, makes a beautiful, warm contrast with the Graphite and Old White mix on the outside of the armoire.*

frottage door

I have noticed that some paint in traditional Swedish decoration ages in a very bold and distinctive way. This is caused partly by how the paint peels away from the surface over time and partly as a result of the old textured paint finishes that were once used. I wanted to achieve such a look for two very old doors at home, which I had already painted Duck Egg Blue. They had great character but I felt this could be more pronounced by using one of my favorite paint techniques, which I call frottage—the name comes from the French *frotter*, meaning to rub. Paint is applied thinly and given texture and character by blotting it with a big sheet of newspaper.

YOU WILL NEED
- Olive paint
- Paint roller tray
- Pages from a large-format newspaper
- Large oval brush
- Clear wax
- 1in (2.5cm) brush, to apply the wax

Tip: Use two colors that are close in tone and of the same family for the base coat and the topcoat, rather than two contrasting ones. Other colors that would work really well are Arles with Primer Red on top, and Aubusson Blue with Paris Grey on top, to stay with the Swedish look.

1 Dilute the paint with water so that it drips when applied to a vertical surface. Lightly crinkle sheets of newspaper, then flatten them out so you are ready for action.

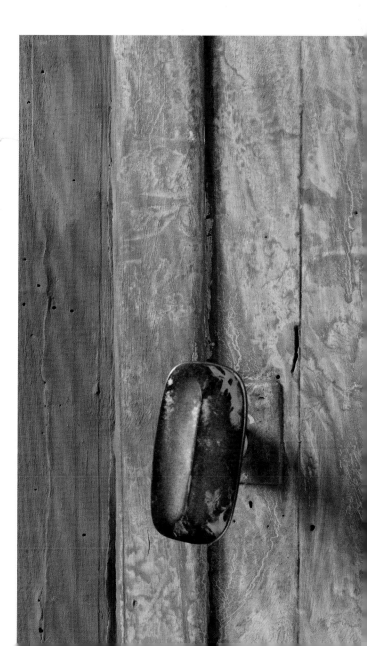

2 Apply the diluted paint to the door with the oval brush, covering an area about the size of a large open newspaper. The paint should be a little transparent and not completely opaque. You need to work quickly so a large brush is essential.

3 As soon as you have finished painting this first section of the door, press a flattened sheet of newspaper up against it. Rub the sheet all over with your hands, applying a moderate amount of pressure.

4 When you remove the paper, the paint underneath will appear uneven and blotchy, as intended. It will still be flat in places, elsewhere it will be textured or it will have disappeared altogether, having been absorbed by the newspaper. Repeat steps 3 and 4 on the rest of the door, using a different sheet of crinkled and flattened newspaper each time, while the edge of the paint is still wet—you want to avoid creating an obvious line.

5 When all the paint is dry, apply clear wax to the entire door using the 1in (2.5cm) brush.

swedish rustic table

There are so many different ways in which paint can age and distress furniture. On really old pieces that have been painted many times and perhaps been cleaned a lot in the past, the paint can become very textured and worn.

I have had this old table for some years. It was covered in a turquoise-blue gloss when I bought it, and I initially painted it Sienna Yellow, a color no longer available. I then thought it would suit this room so much better if it were Scandinavian Pink but that didn't look great. Immediately, I tried Primer Red. Perfect. The tabletop has been painted with a colorwash (see page 106).

(see page 106)

YOU WILL NEED

- Primer Red paint
- Clear wax
- Large oval brush, to apply the wax
- Medium oval brush, to apply the paint
- Plenty of clean, dry, lint-free cloths
- Coarse sandpaper

Tip: Changing your mind about paint colors is so easy with my paint, Chalk Paint®. Simply cover the paint you no longer want with the one you do!

1 While the Scandinavian Pink paint is still a little damp in places (by that I mean, not completely dry all over), apply a generous amount of clear wax with the large oval brush. Don't rub the wax into the surface of the paint. Where the paint is a little damp, the Scandinavian Pink will come off, revealing the yellow underneath.

2 If the weather is cool, leave the wax to dry out a little but if it is warm, follow this step right away. You need to be painting on soft "wet" wax. Apply one solid coat of Primer Red over all the waxed wood with the medium oval brush. Leave for an hour or so, depending on the temperature —I left it for an hour in cool weather.

3 Wipe off the Primer Red with clean, dry cloths—you will need plenty of them, as this is a pretty messy business. Some paint will stay and some will wipe off easily.

4 Rub all over the surface with coarse sandpaper. Vary the pressure you apply, rubbing hard in some places to reveal the colors underneath, including the original turquoise-blue. Brush all over with clear wax, removing any excess with a clean, dry cloth.

painted floor

The floors in the two bedrooms are both pine. A wash of Old White paint has made them look very soft and mellow, and also lightened the rooms considerably. Bedroom floors generally don't need any protection, so I've left these to wear in their own way.

YOU WILL NEED
- Old White paint
- Medium to large brush
- Damp sponge
- Bucket of water

The look is inspired by the traditional Swedish way of painting wooden floors using lye. This very strong alkali made from potash was used with soap on floors to bleach the wood and soften its appearance. My method does not give exactly the same beautiful look but it is a very good alternative, as it is so quick and economical.

Both these floors had never been varnished, stained, or waxed, which is best if you want to paint them because the paint is easily absorbed into the wood. Varnished wood can be treated in the same way but the paint will possibly wear away more easily unless it is lacquered. However, if you're after a worn look, then this technique will be fine.

1 Plan your progress through the room so that you paint the entire floor and don't end up painting yourself into a corner. Starting furthest away from the door as you can, paint the floorboards in small, easy-to-reach sections.

Tip: White is a good floor color, but there are others that also work well, such as Duck Egg Blue, Paris Grey, and Old Ochre. For a dark alternative, try Graphite, Olive, and Aubusson Blue, which look very elegant, especially when lacquered.

2 When you have finished painting a section, wipe over the floorboards with a damp sponge, spreading out the paint until you achieve the look you are after.

3 Move on to the next section, painting and sponging the floorboards in the same way. Make sure that the color is consistent, adding more paint or more water, as appropriate. Have a bucket of water nearby to wash the sponge out and to gather up more water.

Tip: When old wood is painted, sometimes the tannins come through, causing a yellow-brown stain. Test to see if this will happen by painting a section of the floor that is unseen and leave it for a week. If the stain comes through, you will need to seal the whole floor with a clear stain blocker. If you are going to apply a lacquer or varnish, test this in advance, too. The final color may not be as you anticipate.

painted dresser

This large pine dresser in our Normandy house has a history of different paint finishes and styles. At various times, it has been white, blue, and orange but for its latest incarnation I opted for a Swedish rustic look. Inspired by a large built-in dresser which I saw in a Swedish castle many years ago and have loved ever since, I decided to paint the dresser blue and white. However, this combination had no impact at all, so I experimented further and eventually plumped for Château Grey, a greenish earth-brown color, adding some detailing in Old White.

YOU WILL NEED

- Château Grey paint
- Old White paint
- Large oval brush
- Straight edge
- Pencil
- Sketchbook
- Small artist's sable brush, No. 3 or 4
- Mixing tray
- Clear wax
- Clean, dry, lint-free cloth
- Fine sandpaper

1 Paint the entire dresser in Château Grey with the large oval brush, covering the previously painted and waxed wood.

RIGHT *A delicate border of branches and spots in Old White runs along the shelf edges. When rubbed back, some of the previous paint colors become visible.*

2 Measure the depth of the shelf edge and paint one of the complete decorative motifs to fit in a sketchbook. Measure the length of the motif. Draw a very light pencil line along the middle of each shelf edge, then make a pencil dot where each motif should start and finish. This will help to keep them roughly the same size and ensure that the dots are in a straight line.

3 Mix the Old White with a little water, so that it is easier to apply. Press the tip of the bristles of the artist's brush on the side of the mixing tray to make sure that the paint flows from it, then paint the repeat motif along all the shelf edges. To make the thin lines representing the stem, apply the brush very lightly so only its tip makes contact with the wood. To make the leaf shapes, apply the brush firmly, then lightly at the very end, so the brush comes off making a point.

4 Rub clear wax into the entire dresser with a clean, dry cloth, paying special attention to the edges. Spread the wax evenly and allow it to be absorbed into the paint.

5 Rub the fine sandpaper gently along the shelf edges, taking off just a little of the painted design to soften it where necessary and to remove any obvious pencil lines. Apply another coat of wax all over with the same cloth, as above.

Tip: The most important part of painting small decorative designs like this shelf edging is to get the paint consistency right. Too much water and the paint will spread out; too little water and the brush won't be able to pull the paint with it.

decorated drawers

I thought the delicate hand-painted motif on the shelves would give the dresser sufficient focus but the piece still looked to me rather unfinished. This was probably because it needed some Old White on the base for balance.

As I still wanted the decorative motif to be the hero of the piece, I needed something that would not distract the eye from it too much. I opted for a border on the drawers, which is a very simple and powerful way to give a piece of furniture some focus.

ABOVE *The insides of the drawers and cupboards have been painted Scandinavian Pink, complementing the interior of the armoire in the same room (see page 98). Giving emphasis to the exterior of each drawer is a rectangular border in Old White.*

YOU WILL NEED
- Old White paint
- Paris Grey paint
- 1in (25mm) masking tape
- Scissors
- Small bristle brush
- Scissors
- Clear wax
- Clean, dry, lint-free cloth
- Fine sandpaper

Tip: making painted lines the right size and in proportion is very important. Two lines, one finer than the other, are better than one wide one.

1 Stick the outer lines of masking tape on the drawer, using the edges of the drawer as a guide to keep the tape straight. Cut the roll of tape to give a straight edge and stick a length of tape parallel to one of the horizontal outer lines, leaving a gap of about ¼in (6mm) between them. Trim the tape to give a straight edge at the other end and stick it down, leaving the same size gap. Repeat for the second inner line and for the vertical lines. Press the edges of the tape down firmly to make certain no paint seeps underneath.

Tip: Use the paint sparingly. If there is too much on the brush or it is applied too thickly, it may go under the tape, resulting in a messy line.

2 Put a little Old White paint on the small bristle brush and stab and wipe along the gap between the lines of tape. Add a very little amount of Paris Grey in places to vary the color slightly. This will soften the lines of Old White and make them appear more natural.

3 Remove the tape carefully as soon as you have finished painting. Rub clear wax over the drawers with a clean, dry cloth, spreading it evenly and allowing it to be absorbed into the paint. Sand over the lines gently, wearing them away in places so they don't appear too hard-edged.

color wash over wax

To balance the lines on the dresser drawers, I painted around the door panels in Old White, using masking tape to keep the lines straight and protect the paintwork, but I still felt that the panels needed something more. I decided to cover them in a wash of Old White.

YOU WILL NEED

- Old White paint
- Clear wax
- Large round brush, to apply the wax
- Clean, dry, lint-free cloths, to apply the wax and the color wash
- Medium flat brush

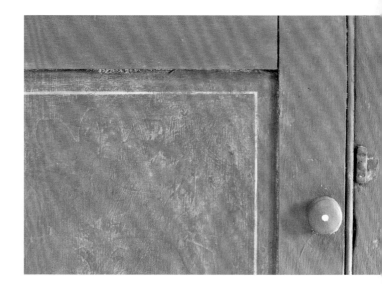

1 Get all your materials ready, as the painting has to follow the waxing immediately, while the wax is still "wet." Apply the wax to the door panels with the large round brush.

2 Spread the wax evenly across the panel with a clean, dry cloth, wiping away any excess.

3 Add water to the Old White paint—it should be thin enough to be a little translucent. If the paint is too watery, the wax will repel it; if it is too dry, you will not be able to spread it. Paint the diluted Old White over the whole panel with the flat brush. Have a little water and paint to hand so you can easily adjust the mix.

4 As soon as you have finished painting, start rubbing and wiping with a clean, dry cloth to make a wash of color. Apply more clear wax, as above, if an area looks too white.

wall sconce

This cast-bronze wall sconce is one of a pair. Although I found them in France, I could see them being used to stunning effect in a Swedish-style interior. Their beautiful shape is pure rococo—sinuous and elegant—but the bronze color was just a little heavy.

Any metal is easy to paint with my paint, Chalk Paint®, even if it is much shinier and brighter than this bronze, which is particularly mellow. I chose to paint over the sconce in cool colors, primarily Paris Grey, then wiped away some of the paint to reveal the metal underneath. This lightened the overall look and created a playful contrast.

YOU WILL NEED

● Paint in cool colors, such as Paris Grey, Olive, Château Grey, Old Violet, Duck Egg Blue, Louis Blue

● Small oval brush

● Clean, dry, lint-free cloth

RIGHT I tried out several colors on the sconces. From left to right: Old White, Old Violet, Olive, Paris Grey, and Graphite. Graphite and Old White contrast strongly with the sheen of the metal and reduce its warmth and patina.

1 Experiment with several different colors on the metal, painting them on with a brush and removing them with a clean, dry cloth. Using sample pots of paint will make this simple and inexpensive to do.

RIGHT *I fixed this sconce to the middle of one of the Country Grey painted panels at the bottom of the stairs and added some pale cream candles. Both sconces were painted primarily in Paris Grey, which picked up the colors in the rest of the room. Their very ornate, rococo style works particularly well with the restrained, classic painted lines on the wall.*

Tip: All metallic gold colors are warm, so they work very well with cooler colors, such as blues, grays, and greens, and they make an agreeable balance for the eye.

2 Once you have decided on your color combinations and roughly where you wish them to be, paint them on, wiping off some of the color with a clean, dry cloth as you go, to reveal some of the bronze underneath. Along the curves of the foliage, slide a finger along instead, to wipe off the paint.

3 As wall sconces are rarely handled, they don't need to be waxed for protection, and the contrast between the painted areas and the bronze can be easily maintained.

faux marble tabletop Traditional classic

Swedish interiors, which many people love, often include decorative paintwork inspired by the lines and colors of marble. However, pieces of furniture treated in this way were very often painted in a quite fanciful and decorative style rather than trying to imitate marble exactly.

I've chosen to show my interpretation of this technique, which has to be done on a flat surface, on a little, round pedestal table. You need a dark paint for the base color and a light one for the top coat so there is enough contrast to show the ring marks made by the denatured alcohol (methylated spirits) rejecting the paint mix.

YOU WILL NEED

- Dark paint color, such as Aubusson Blue or Olive
- Light paint color, such as Old White
- Medium oval brush
- Decoupage varnish, such as Annie Sloan All-in-one Decoupage Glue and Varnish)
- Paint roller tray
- Sponge paint roller
- Denatured alcohol (methylated spirits)
- Small, flat bristle brush, to spatter the denatured alcohol
- Small, flat bristle brush, to spatter the paint
- Clear wax
- Medium flat brush, to apply the wax
- Clean, dry, lint-free cloths

LEFT *This finished marble-effect pedestal table had a base color of Olive, with Old White on top.*

RIGHT *The chair has been painted in French Linen and upholstered with one of the old monogrammed linen sheets given to me by my neighbor (see page 36).*

1 Paint the table with a dark color—I used Aubusson Blue here. Mix Old White paint and decoupage varnish together in roughly equal measures in a paint roller tray. With a clean, dry brush, paint this mix over the Aubusson Blue, spreading it so it appears a little translucent and you can see the base color through it.

2 Using a dry sponge paint roller, roll over the surface, so the paint and varnish mix is even and like a translucent film on top of the dark base color.

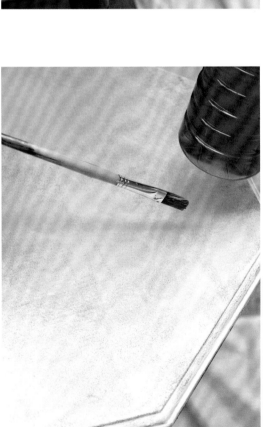

3 While the surface is still wet, take a small, flat bristle brush and spatter the surface with denatured alcohol (methylated spirits). This quickly forms ring spots but they are very faint at this stage.

4 Use a fresh, dry sponge roller (or clean and dry off the one already used) and roll it over the tabletop gently but firmly. This will lift off the paint where the alcohol has formed rings. Roll the sponge over several times to remove the maximum amount of paint and make the effect more striking. Be aware, though, that if you do this too many times, the rings will start to blur together. If there aren't enough spotty marks, then spatter on more denatured alcohol and roll again.

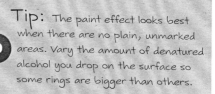

Tip: The paint effect looks best when there are no plain, unmarked areas. Vary the amount of denatured alcohol you drop on the surface so some rings are bigger than others.

5 Dilute some Old White paint with just enough water so that it remains opaque and can be easily spattered. This will give the marbling effect a little more depth. Avoid spattering the paint all over the surface—leave some areas either free of Old White altogether or less densely covered.

6 Roll a clean, dry sponge roller over the white spots, to flatten them and make them more varied in size and shape. When the paint is completely dry, apply a coat of clear wax with a brush, wiping away any excess with a clean, dry cloth.

country

As my Normandy house is in the French countryside, it suits being decorated in the country style, although some rooms are a little grander than others. Grand is not a word that can be used to describe the kitchen, though. Like many old farmhouse kitchens, it is a meeting place, with both the front and back doors leading directly into it. It's where we eat, cook, and gather, where we take off our boots and where we sit by the fire in the evenings. The kitchen is the room where country style is best illustrated, but it also appears in the French and Swedish chapters—the walls in the bedrooms were plastered with mud and then painted, and the floors were painted.

Country style has developed out of practicality, with function definitely coming before style. It is a weathered, worn, and natural look, with worn, washed, and faded painted wood, limed oak, and rough walls. It can appear natural and earthy with whites and neutrals or whites and grays, but it can also be quite colorful. With a style that has come straight from the farm, bold colors, such as strong reds, bright greens, and blues, suit it well. For my country kitchen, I have chosen softer worn and faded colors rather than bright ones, although I do have a hankering to use some Emperor's Silk—my pure red—somewhere!

sanded kitchen chairs

I bought this set of six sturdy chairs with rush seats mainly for use in the kitchen as dining chairs (you can see them with the painted teak table on page 125), but they do get moved around to other parts of the house. The traditional design on the back of the chairs is typical of Brittany, which neighbors my area of Normandy. Although quite modern and abstract, the design manages to have a country look as well.

As in so many very old farmhouses, with their small windows, the kitchen is generally dark. I needed to introduce some color to brighten it up. It is a common misunderstanding that when a room is dark, it should be painted white, but white can just look gray and dull in the shadows. Painting strong pastels, on the other hand, will make a room look lively and bright.

YOU WILL NEED
- Duck Egg Blue paint
- Louis Blue paint
- Château Grey paint
- Old Violet paint
- Versailles paint
- Provence paint
- Medium oval brush
- Fine or medium sandpaper
- Clear wax
- Clean, dry, lint-free cloths

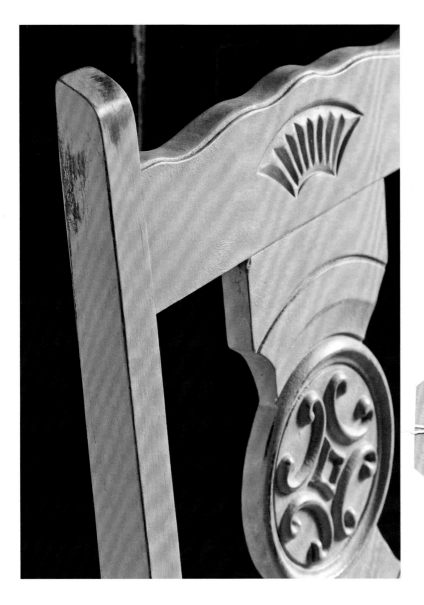

RIGHT *Before starting on my chairs and the kitchen decoration, I made a color plan. The predominant colors for the whole room are cool: Duck Egg Blue and Louis Blue on the ceiling, with the kitchen cabinets in Duck Egg Blue. These are set against the warm soft plaster-pink of Antoinette on the walls. I continued with the cool color palette for the chairs, adding Château Grey, Old Violet, Versailles, and Provence, so they would work in the kitchen but also in any room in the house.*

LEFT *Each chair has been treated in a different way. On some, the tops have been sanded back; on others, the legs. Sanding back to the wood adds to the charm.*

Tip: Rush seats are easily painted. These were covered with slightly watered-down paint in the same color used for the wood, and then waxed.

1 Remove the chair seats and paint them separately (see Tip). Using the medium oval brush, paint each chair all over with your chosen color, covering the wood well but not as thickly as in the Chipped Paint Cabinet (see page 44). Make the brushstrokes go in all directions over any carving, to make certain everything is covered. Allow to dry.

2 Rub the sandpaper all over the chair. As the sanding is done before the waxing, more paint is taken off, so take care not to be too enthusiastic! This method is quite dusty so it is best done outside or where the dust won't matter.

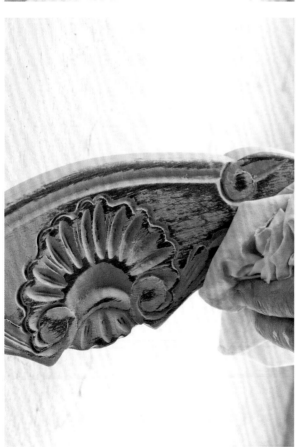

3 Wipe the sanding dust away, then apply clear wax all over with a clean, dry cloth. This will make some of the sanded paintwork more apparent. Repeat all the steps for the remaining chairs.

painted teak table

The table in our kitchen is used for many things, from preparing and eating food to working on the computer. It was given to us by a friend, who had acquired it many years ago from a school that was clearing out its old chemistry labs. Being exactly the same length as the old pew that runs along the wall, it was the perfect addition, except for its color, which was rather too dark and formal.

I decided that covering the table with a wash would be a good idea, lightening it but also retaining some of its wonderful patina. This proved a lot more difficult than I had thought, though. I struggled to get the paint to cover and it was far too easy to wipe it off. My husband took a look and said cheerily, "Ah, you're painting the teak table." Then the penny dropped as to why the painting was so hard.

Teak is an extremely oily wood, perfect for boat decks, outdoor furniture, and chemistry tables, where the wood will not absorb chemicals and cross-pollute. It is so oily that, despite the age of the table and the fact that I had never applied any wax or oil to it, the wood was repelling the paint. Armed with this knowledge, I persevered with my painting and won!

YOU WILL NEED
- Old White paint
- Medium oval brush
- Clean, dry, lint-free cloths, to rub in the paint and to apply the wax
- Clear wax

Tip: The natural oiliness of teak may vary in a single piece of furniture, making it impossible to control the opacity of the paint, no matter how much you apply.

ABOVE *The finish was a beautiful, uneven wash of white. In places translucent, in others opaque, the paint highlights the table's many nicks, dents, and scratches, giving it extra character and texture.*

1 Add a little water to the Old White paint, if necessary, to allow it to glide on easily. Working in areas of an arm's length, paint on the first coat, pushing the paint into the wood, even when the paint becomes quite dry.

2 Once an area is completed, take a clean, dry cloth and wipe off the paint, rubbing it into the wood as you go, to help the teak absorb the paint. I found the absorption rate was a little uneven, with more paint being absorbed in some areas than others. Repeat steps 1 and 2 for the entire table. Let the paint dry for a few hours.

3 To make the surface more even, apply a second coat of paint, diluted with a little more water. Wipe a dry cloth over the surface, as you did in step 2. You will see how the oil in the wood still repels the paint but don't be put off. Leave the paint to dry overnight.

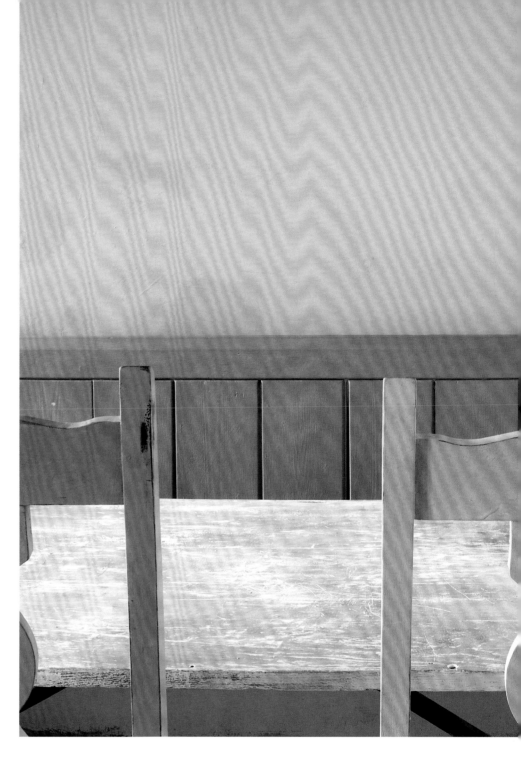

4 Once the paint is completely dry, apply clear wax with a clean, dry cloth. Use circular movements but be sensitive about the amount of pressure you apply—if you are too firm, you will remove all the paint. In places, the paint will appear translucent or disappear altogether; in others, it will stay opaque.

painting rough walls

As with many old houses in France, the ground-floor walls of our house are built of stone, while the upper levels are made from a mix of mud and straw. Some of the wall in what is now our bedroom was in a very poor condition, as it had been left unattended for years—chickens had once roosted there, then some owls moved in! It was originally made from a mix of mud, cow manure, and straw, and we followed tradition when we repaired it, although we omitted the manure. This has given us a sturdy wall but with some fine cracks. To cover these and lighten the overall effect, I chose to paint it over with diluted Old White.

I had to be careful not to overbrush because the paint would end up being discolored by the mud. However, as the paint was absorbed and dried quickly, it was easy to go back to an area and give an extra coat of paint. This technique can also be used on other absorbent and uneven surfaces, such as brick and limestone.

YOU WILL NEED
- Old White paint
- Bucket
- Wooden stick or brush, to stir the water and paint
- Wide, flat bristle brush, to apply the water and the paint
- Clean, dry, lint-free cloth

1 Pour the Old White paint into the bucket—a 1-liter can of paint will cover roughly 140sq ft (13sq m) before you add the water (see step 2), which will give you almost double the coverage.

2 Using the wooden stick, stir in water to make the paint thin enough to paint on easily but not so thin that it is runny and won't cover well. You will probably end up adding about 1 liter (2 pints) of water.

3 Paint the wall generously with water—this will make applying the Old White much easier, as the water will draw the paint into the wall.

ABOVE *The fine cracks in the wall and the uneven surface of the mud and straw add real character to the bedroom.*

4 Brush the diluted Old White on the wall, stabbing with the bristles to make sure the entire surface is covered.

5 Paint a coat of diluted Old White over the wooden lintel, then wipe it over with a clean, dry cloth, covering up the dark contrasting color but leaving the texture of the wood still visible.

rustic washed table

My very old kitchen table, with its well-marked pitch-pine top, had experienced a few years of wear and tear, which had made the wood look rather too characterful. To lighten it and clean it up, removing the many stains and scratches but without losing the grain of the wood, I gave the table a wash of Old White paint. The finished table still retains its character but there is a refined elegance about it now, reminiscent of Swedish painted furniture.

YOU WILL NEED
- Old White paint
- 2in (5cm) flat or oval brush [please check size]
- Plenty of clean, dry, lint-free cloths

1 Apply the paint with a flat or oval brush, working in the direction of the wood grain. You may need to add a little water to the paint so that it flows easily and can be more readily absorbed. Work in small areas at a time so that the paint doesn't completely dry.

2 Before the paint has time to dry, wipe it off with a circular motion using a clean, dry cloth—pressing hard as you wipe will remove more paint than pressing lightly. Experiment with brushing and wiping several times until you work out the right thickness of paint and pressure to apply with the cloth for the desired look.

ABOVE *A color wash applied to new wood that is smooth and clean, and perhaps with a yellow hue, will look quite different when painted onto old wood that has become textured and paler over the years. The amount of paint that is absorbed also varies according to the type of wood, so don't expect your table to look like the one in the photograph unless the wood is very similar. Other paint colors that work well for this effect are Duck Egg Blue and Paris Grey.*

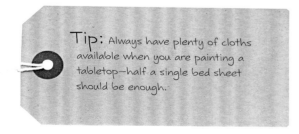

Tip: Always have plenty of cloths available when you are painting a tabletop—half a single bed sheet should be enough.

ceiling and rafters

The previous owners of our old house in Normandy had tacked a ramshackle and unattractive arrangement of hardboard sheets onto the kitchen ceiling. When we took them down, we not only found a large layer of hard, caked mud (this was the traditional material for making floors) but also that some of the original rafters were either missing or rotten and had to be replaced.

After this work had taken place, I was left with a ceiling made up of a mix of old, black-stained rafters and some new ones. Both the ceiling and the rafters had to be painted. I decided against white because that would have left the room looking rather cold. Color, on the other hand, would brighten things up. Blues and greens are recessive, which means that they help to give a room a feeling of space. I opted for Duck Egg Blue paint for the rafters and Louis Blue for the ceiling, both of which were already used in the kitchen: Duck Egg Blue on the cabinets, the interior of a cupboard, and one of the chairs, and Louis Blue on another chair.

1 Using a sponge roller, which has a cleaner edge than a woolly roller, apply the Louis Blue to the ceiling. I chose this color because it looks like a summer sky and also has depth. Go right into the edge of the rafters—it doesn't matter if you get paint on them.

YOU WILL NEED
- Duck Egg Blue paint
- Louis Blue paint
- Sponge roller
- Large flat brush

2 Paint the rafters with the flat brush—most of these rafters are old, very gnarled, and uneven, so they required a lot of painting. Use the flat end of the brush to get into the join between the ceiling and the rafters. There is no need to apply any wax or varnish, so the end result is a ceiling with a very matte finish.

Tip: When painting a ceiling and rafters, use two colors that are very close in tone, such as the Duck Egg Blue and Louis Blue that I used here.

limed oak look

The beams and the basic structure of old farmhouses were traditionally made of oak because this wood hardens with age and becomes stronger. To preserve the wood and keep the bugs at bay, the oak was whitewashed with lime every year—the caustic nature of the lime in the whitewash killed the bugs.

Oak is a rough wood with a deep grain that traps paint, which is why very old whitewashed oak often has a soft gray/silvery look about it. Over the years, the whitewash would gather in the recesses, creating an effect that is now known as limed oak. It's a beautiful look, as it shows up the quite distinctive and decorative grain of the wood. In contrast, 20th-century oak furniture has often been stained and varnished to a dull brown, which does not bring out the best of the grain at all.

Oak furniture covered in a heavy, modern varnish will need to be stripped before being painted, otherwise the paint won't be able to enter the grain. However, it is surprising how some stained and/or varnished oak still retains its grainy texture, so I always test a piece first by painting a small area that won't be visible. If the paint enters the grain, then I don't need to strip it.

YOU WILL NEED
- Old White paint
- Medium oval brush
- Clean, dry, lint-free cloths
- Clear wax
- 1in (2.5cm) brush, to apply the wax (optional)

Tip: Old White is the perfect color to use with oak but other colors that work well are blues and grays, in particular, Paris Grey and Duck Egg Blue, which give the wood a silvery, bleached look.

1 Paint over the surface with the oval brush, a small area at a time, so that none of the paint really dries before you reach step 2.

ABOVE *I first painted this sideboard about 20 years ago when it was in my old country kitchen in England, before we moved into town. Since then, it has been transferred to my French farmhouse kitchen, where it fits the space perfectly. The paint has worn away pleasingly in places that have been touched a lot, notably the drawers and the top of the door on the left.*

2 As the paint dries, gently wipe it off so that it is just left behind in the grain. If the paint is too dry, add a spit of water to the cloth. Don't remove too much of the paint because the wax, applied in step 3, will lighten the paint and give the desired transparent effect.

3 If there is any carving, apply clear wax with a brush, so that you can reach the more inaccessible areas. Otherwise, use a clean, dry cloth. Work on a small area at a time, wiping off any excess with a cloth as you go to avoid a build-up of wax.

modern
contemporary

Nowadays, with more and more modern pieces of furniture available from the 1950s and 1960s, it is important to paint them in an appropriate way. Pieces can be painted in a retro way, meaning that we look back to the time after the Second World War when there was a boom in technology and use of color after years of austerity. English Yellow, Paris Grey, and Louis Blue are retro colors, along with Barcelona Orange and Olive.

Alternatively, painting can be modern and architectural where there's minimal decoration and large slabs of color are used in a room, as well as painting just one wall in a different color to the other walls. Stripes take a more central role in decoration and we have become more and more aware of clear, simple color.

When I went to art school in the late 1960s, many of my tutors were painting abstract expressionist and field paintings inspired by the hugely influential New York school of artists, which included Mark Rothko, Morris Louis, Barnett Newman, and Frank Stella, to name a few. These artists used strong and simple geometric shapes, stripes, and targets to describe, play, and emphasize colors and tone and the way they look next to each other. This has stayed with me and has continued to play an important part in my design and color choices. The colors can be deep, such as Burgundy, Aubusson Blue, and Florence, with flashes of bright color such as English Yellow, Arles, and Pure for maximum contrast.

BELOW *Choosing the colors that work together should be done in advance, before you are tempted to begin painting. Aim for a group of some dark and light neutrals, many cool colors, and just a few warm colors. I repeated each color several times, especially the neutrals and cool colors. I started with a smaller group of colors, but found I added a few more as I went. Sample pots are a good way to use a lot of colors economically.*

striped stairs

This is a modern staircase comprising 14 stairs, which was fairly unremarkable, rather dark, and generally needed cheering up. It was inspired by a staircase which caught my eye on the Pinterest website because of its wobbly, uneven nature. Although all that was needed here was a series of horizontal lines, it was a difficult undertaking. Making certain that the rhythm of loud, quiet, deep, and high colors works well requires time and planning.

Remember that the cool colors—blues, greens, and quiet Old Violet—are used more frequently than the few lines of the hot, bright colors. There are only about nine or ten stripes of these hot colors, yet they dominate over the cooler stripes.

YOU WILL NEED

● A good selection of paint (see right for guidance on color choices)
● 2in (5cm) flat synthetic brush

1 Each stripe of paint is not only a little wobbly but is also of a different width and some are on the step and the riser too, so blurring the definition of the stairs giving it an interesting twist.

2 This detail of newel post shows a different technique—lime washing on oak (see page 132), which makes a great contrast to the colorful stripes.

Tip: Use a flat synthetic brush which can easily get into edges and corners. Don't overload the brush to avoid paint pooling and making raised edges.

smooth and shiny bureau

This bureau probably dates from the 1950s and I felt it would benefit from a slick and shiny modern look, rather than a distressed and shabby one. I love this style of writing desk, the main reason being it is a great opportunity to create a bright interior and make some surprising color contrasts. The inside of the bureau is now rather like the red silk lining of a tuxedo.

YOU WILL NEED

- Graphite paint
- Emperor's Silk paint
- Barcelona Orange paint
- Synthetic wide, flat brush
- Wooden stick, to mix the paint
- Paint roller tray
- Clear wax
- Clean, dry, lint-free cloth, for polishing

RIGHT *One of the most enjoyable and intriguing things about working with color is the way in which any color will appear to change depending on the color alongside it. Each one will be given certain characteristics, making it appear lighter, duller, or brighter. Red, for example, will look dazzling if placed alongside any color within the opposing segment on the color wheel, such as bright turquoise-blue or green (see page 15). On the other hand, if red is placed alongside black, the effect is the exact opposite. This is because these colors are similar in tone—to test this, half-close your eyes and look at the black and the red side by side; you will see that both colors almost disappear, with neither appearing darker than the other. Graphite next to English Yellow on this bureau would have made a powerful combination because of the high contrast of color. The impact of Graphite with a more muted color with less contrast would be much less.*

LEFT *My inspiration for the red and black color combination came from a vintage French print of an advertisement for silk stockings. I re-created the stunning tomato-red by mixing Emperor's Silk with some Barcelona Orange, giving just the right glow.*

1 Make sure that the paint will go on smoothly by seeing if it drips easily from the brush. If it doesn't, add some water and stir well.

2 Paint Graphite all over the exterior of the bureau with the wide, flat brush. As you go, brush out the paint so there are no brush marks—a few will be fine, as these will flatten as the paint dries. Paint a second coat, then let dry thoroughly.

3 Mix the Emperor's Silk with some Barcelona Orange, a little at a time, in the roller tray with the wooden stick, until you get the desired shade of tomato-red. Paint the inside of the bureau and the drop-down lid. Paint on a second coat, then let dry thoroughly.

4 Using the medium, flat brush, apply clear wax all over the bureau, including the inside, making certain that it is completely absorbed into the paint. Apply a second coat of wax, again allowing it to be well absorbed. The next day, polish the bureau all over with a cloth—leaving the wax overnight makes it easier to polish.

modern stripes

Painting stripes using a mix of colors is much harder than it looks. I've found that the best way of creating them is to paint on alternate broad stripes, which gives the paint time to dry before you paint the stripe alongside, followed by thinner stripes on top. If you paint two colors side by side that don't quite work, you can always paint a different-colored stripe on top to separate them.

We are all very familiar with stripes on fabric but having them painted on furniture is a decidedly modern look. For the base colors on this marble-topped chest of drawers, I chose a series of predominantly bright, clear shades, like children's candy, and all of a similar tone. I then used whites and dark neutrals between them to intensify the colors and provide contrast. A similar contemporary but more sophisticated look could be achieved using grays and pale browns with whites.

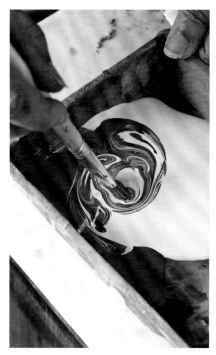

ABOVE *To lighten a bright color, such as Emperor's Silk, which is a clear red, you will need to add a clean white, such as Pure, which is also soft. The brighter the white, the cleaner the look. Establish the paint proportions by experimenting until you get the exact shade you are after, then make up a batch big enough to paint the desired area.*

YOU WILL NEED

- Sketchbook and sample pots
- Provence paint
- Arles paint
- Emperor's Silk paint
- Pure paint
- Old Violet paint
- Graphite paint
- Olive paint
- Fine sandpaper
- Clean, dry, lint-free cloth
- Flat brushes of various widths
- Thick card

1 Decide on your colors before you start painting. I made a drawing first of the chest of drawers, then painted on stripes in different permutations—sample pots make this really easy and inexpensive to do—to establish which colors would work best together and in which order. For my base stripes, I chose Provence, Arles, Old Violet, and a bright clear pink, which I made by mixing Emperor's Silk and Pure.

LEFT *Painting stripes in different widths is made a great deal easier if you use a range of chisel-ended brushes.*

2 If your piece of furniture is heavily varnished, sand it very lightly to take off the high shine. Although my paints stick to everything, I felt that this chest of drawers was so shiny that a little help was needed. Wipe over the furniture with a clean, slightly damp cloth to remove the dust.

3 Start by painting the front of the chest in broad stripes, covering the wood completely. Paint alternate stripes so that you are not painting next to a wet edge. Continue painting the sides and the back of the chest, if necessary.

4 Use a piece of thick card to make a straight edge, where one color stripe meets the next.

ABOVE *Using a piece of card to make a straight edge, I painted over the Provence with Emperor's Silk, creating a band with the Provence either side. As the turquoise and the red are similar in tone, I kept their stripes about the same width but then added thinner stripes of Pure, Graphite, and the darker-toned Olive.*

5 Use a piece of thick card as a guide to paint thinner stripes in Graphite, Pure, and Olive over the broader stripes. You will generally find that darker paint colors need to be thinner than bright, light colors.

painted rug

Floors are easy to paint, whether they are concrete or wood—simply use a sponge roller, with a brush for the edges. Depending on the type of floor and the color you choose, you will need either one or two coats of paint, plus a final coat of floor lacquer as a sealant.

Painting a rug is a bit of extra fun and a cheeky solution when you despair of finding a real rug in the right size, color, and design for your newly painted floor. After painting this floor with two coats of Old Ochre, I felt it needed a little something to give it focus but instead of holding out in my search for the perfect rug, I decided to paint one. Drawing around a blanket meant that I could get a very natural shape, so that the "rug" looks real.

YOU WILL NEED
- Old White paint
- French Linen paint
- Blanket, to use as a template
- Pencil
- Large, flat-ended brush
- 1in (2.5cm) brush
- Clean, dry, lint-free cloth
- Floor lacquer
- Lacquer brush

1 Take a blanket and fold it to the size you want for your painted rug. Lay it in position on the floor.

2 Draw around the blanket lightly in pencil, following its slightly uneven outline—the pencil line will be covered by the paint.

3 Holding the flat-ended brush at right angles to the floor, paint on Old White, following the pencil line but covering it, and allowing the odd wobble or curve, so that it is like the outline of a fabric rug. Paint the outside of the rectangle first, then fill it in. Let it dry.

RIGHT *This is such an easy way to trick the eye! From afar, the rug looks like the real thing. Only closer inspection reveals that it is, in fact, painted! And if in time the paint becomes too scuffed, it's very easy to paint a new rug.*

4 Dilute the French Linen with a little water. With the 1in (2.5cm) brush, paint a narrow band that loosely follows the edges of the rug, about 2in (5cm) in. (If you don't feel confident about doing this, draw a pencil line first as a guide, covering it as you paint.) Pull the brush along slowly and deliberately, dabbing off any excess paint with a clean, dry cloth, so that the band has added interest and is not completely flat. When the paint becomes too opaque, add a little more water. Let the paint dry, then cover the entire rug with a coat of floor lacquer, to seal it.

hot and clashing colors

This bed is a traditional Breton-style piece of furniture, with simple carvings that have their roots in Celtic design. With such a bold design, I could have simply painted the bed in Old White for it to look effective. However, the patterns reminded me particularly of American abstract art of the 1960s, as well as some more contemporary art, with their bright and unexpected combinations of colors. I felt that this bed was the ideal piece for me to go really bright.

Sometimes people look at my colors, though, and would think that this wouldn't be possible, but it is. Making colors look bright is simply a matter of combining them in the right way. This project is therefore more about working with color than paint techniques.

Although all the windows in my Normandy house face south, this bedroom, formerly the dairy for the farm, has larger windows, so it is even lighter than all the other rooms. More light means that brighter colors can be used, which is perfect as this house doesn't get frequent strong sun, which would make very vibrant colors glaring.

YOU WILL NEED

- Barcelona Orange paint
- Emperor's Silk paint
- Pure paint
- Emile paint
- Old Violet paint
- Antibes Green paint
- Florence paint
- Greek Blue paint
- Provence paint
- Olive paint
- Large, oval brush
- Paint roller trays
- Narrow, oval brush
- ½in (12mm) flat-ended artist's brush
- Clear wax
- 1in (2.5cm) oval brush, to apply the wax
- Clean, dry, lint-free cloths

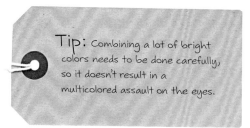

Tip: Combining a lot of bright colors needs to be done carefully, so it doesn't result in a multicolored assault on the eyes.

1 Paint the whole bed in Barcelona Orange with the large, oval brush. Mix Emperor's Silk and Pure together in a paint roller tray, to create a bright pink. Apply this to the narrow bands of decorative molding with the narrow, oval brush. Let the paint dry.

LEFT *Hot colors are normally used quite sparingly, as a little of them goes a long way (see Striped Stairs, page 136). However, I wanted to create as much impact as I could with this project. I started off with a "bed" of hot, vibrant Barcelona Orange, then picked out the linear molding in a bright pink, made by mixing Emperor's Silk and Pure. The clashing of the pink next to the orange helps to give the bed its frisson. Painted over the entire bed, the Barcelona Orange projects forward, in direct contrast with the carved areas, painted in a variety of deep, cool colors, which recede. If the bed were primarily blue, with the carved sections in hot oranges and pink, the overall effect would be a great deal quieter.*

2 Using the artist's brush, paint each of the chevron shapes in the star-shaped carvings a different color. The blues and greens that I used were made by mixing varying proportions of Antibes Green with Florence, and Greek Blue with Provence.

3 Paint the "target" carvings in the same colors as the star shapes, but use Olive for the middle circle. Let the paint dry.

4 Apply clear wax all over the bed with the wax brush. The wax will make the colors very slightly darker, especially when first applied. When it dries out a little, you will find it has not darkened the paint as much as the initial change.

5 Rub the wax into the paint with a clean, dry cloth, so it is fully absorbed. For a matte look, do not polish the wax. If you want a shiny look, polish it now and also the next day.

ABOVE *The Paris Grey on the wall is a quiet, cool color but its slight blue tinge helps to make the Barcelona Orange on the bed pop out—blue and orange are complementary colors, meaning they are opposite from each other on the color wheel (see pages 14–15). The cool neutral aspect of the Paris Grey also helps to quieten the bed colors a little.*

typographical chest of drawers

There is a huge interest in typography today, although it's really not surprising, as billboards, signs, and notices are to be seen everywhere. Many people are very knowledgeable about fonts and appreciate the beauty of old advertisements with their old-fashioned typefaces. These are now being used to decorate a lot of furniture. Inspired by several such pieces that I'd seen on social-media sites, I decided to create my own.

I'd had this eccentric, probably handmade piece of furniture in my studio for many years. It had obviously once been used in a garage, as it was covered in oil, and hammer and saw marks. After sealing and painting it, I used it to store my brushes and drawing materials. For a long time, though, I had my eye on it as possible storage for important papers, keys, and souvenirs in the main part of the house.

The eight drawers of different depths suggested to me lines of text, so I chose to decorate them with the first lines of James Joyce's "Ulysses." I love the unusual combination of words and the different shapes I make with my mouth when I speak them. The chest now stands at the top of the stairs, as the writing on the fourth drawer suggests.

ABOVE *My drawer letters are created out of sticky plastic letters used to make signs, and are available in a range of different sizes. I have actually used the letters as a resist to the paint, and peeled them off when the paint is dry. I chose a combination of French Linen and Old White because I like the sepia look they create together.*

YOU WILL NEED

- Old White paint
- French Linen paint
- Soft flat brush
- Pencil and paper
- Sticky letters for making signs (I used three different heights: 3in/75mm, 1¾in/47mm, and 1½in/35mm)
- Oval bristle brush
- Clear wax
- Brush, to apply the wax
- Clean, dry, lint-free cloths
- Coarse sandpaper

1 Remove the drawers and paint them and the carcass of the chest in Old White—this will be the color of the letters. Apply the paint smoothly with the soft, flat brush, so you don't create a lot of texture and the letters will stick down well. Cover the handles with paint, too. Let the paint dry.

2 Write down your chosen words on paper, and work out which ones you want for each drawer and the size of the letters. Write the final version on the drawers. For me, this involved a certain amount of trial and error, as the words, the letter size, and the drawers were all different sizes. When happy with their position, stick the letters in place—it is easy to stick and remove them a few times before the glue becomes less effective.

LEFT *The letters are not perfectly straight, or even perfectly aligned and centered, but they are balanced enough and convey just the right amount of idiosyncrasy. When I waxed the drawers, I used a brush that had a little bit of red paint on it. This gave a blush to a few of the words, adding to the interest. The mismatching metal handles also contribute to the uniqueness of the piece. I painted directly over them and sanded them lightly, so that some of the original metal shows through.*

3 Once the letters are in place and firmly stuck down, paint the drawers in French Linen with the oval bristle brush, stippling the letters with fairly dry paint. If the paint is wet and you use the normal brushing technique, paint can go under the letters and spoil them. If this happens, just repaint and try again. Leave the paint to dry.

4 Once the paint is dry, carefully peel off each letter. If any French Linen has seeped under a letter, touch it up with some Old White.

5 Use the brush to apply clear wax all over the drawers and carcass, wiping off any excess with a clean, dry cloth as you go.

6 As this was a very old and roughly made piece of furniture, a little sanding seemed appropriate. Rub coarse sandpaper lightly over the surface, including the handles, to soften the look.

painted contemporary chair

This angular and contemporary chair had been waiting a very long time in its undyed calico for me to be inspired, and it was not until I began to work on my modern room that I had the idea of painting it. The design I chose for the seat and back of the chair is an homage to those mid-20th-century American artists who played around with strong and simple geometric shapes, stripes, and targets to emphasize colors and tones and the different way they looked next to each other.

I chose a deep receding color—Aubusson Blue—for the main part of the chair, with Barcelona Orange and Florence, as well as Florence lightened with Old White for the stripes. Orange and blue are complementary colors (see page 15) so they pop out against each other, which makes the orange appear particularly bright. This turns the chair into a real statement piece for the room. If the blue were as vivid as the orange, that is, of the same tone, the effect would be rather dazzling and startling, as the eye would find it difficult to rest on both colors.

YOU WILL NEED

- Aubusson Blue paint
- Barcelona Orange paint
- Florence paint
- Old White paint, to lighten the Florence
- Medium, flat brush
- Clear wax
- Medium, oval brush, to apply the wax
- Clean, dry, lint-free cloths
- Masking tape
- Scissors
- Flat artist's brush, to paint the stripes

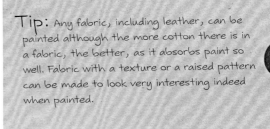

Tip: Any fabric, including leather, can be painted although the more cotton there is in a fabric, the better, as it absorbs paint so well. Fabric with a texture or a raised pattern can be made to look very interesting indeed when painted.

Tip: Check your chosen color combinations before you paint to see what effect the texture and color of the fabric will have on the paint color.

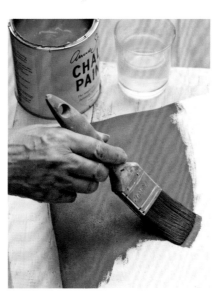

1 For the purposes of photography, I am working here on a drop-in seat for a chair. Apply the Aubusson Blue all over the fabric with the medium, flat brush. Have a glass of water at your side, so you can dip your brush in it from time to time. This will keep the paint thin enough to be absorbed into the fabric. Since the paint will be absorbed unevenly because of the upholstery underneath, you will need to adjust the thickness of the paint constantly. Two coats are best for an even coverage.

After being waxed and polished all over, the painted calico fabric looks and feels like soft leather. The 1960s sideboard behind is painted in Pure, with bright clashing colors on the edges. The Graphite wall has also been coated with clear wax and buffed so that it shines.

2 When the paint is dry, apply a coat of clear wax with the wax brush, wiping it with a clean, dry cloth as you go to achieve an even coverage. For a shiny surface, polish the wax. The shine will make the fabric look and feel like leather.

3 When the wax is dry, cut strips of masking tape to use as a straight edge and place them carefully in parallel lines over the chair seat and back, leaving varying gaps between them. Paint between the lines of tape with Barcelona Orange, Florence, and Florence lightened with Old white, using the flat artist's bristle brush.

monoprint table

As the word suggests, monoprints are one-offs. They have a way of giving paint luminosity and a translucence that you don't get with a painting. They also have a spontaneity, as the different colors flatten and lift and merge into one another in a chance and interesting way.

I have used the simplest form of monoprinting here, which is to paint on paper and print with that, but metal, lino, or soft plastic tiles would also work. Using non-porous materials means you can paint on them and also remove the paint because it is not absorbed. The resulting patterns can be very rich and quite unique. The advantage of paper is that it's easy to find and gives you flexibility.

With my table, I reprinted several times to achieve an overall pattern, and each time I printed, the pattern was just a little bit different. My inspiration came from those rather splashy fabric designs from the 1950s, with their bright colors and abstract vivacity that made them so exciting.

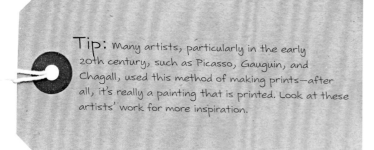

Tip: Many artists, particularly in the early 20th century, such as Picasso, Gauguin, and Chagall, used this method of making prints—after all, it's really a painting that is printed. Look at these artists' work for more inspiration.

YOU WILL NEED
- Duck Egg Blue paint
- Burgundy paint
- English Yellow paint
- Olive paint
- Large, oval brush
- White paper
- 1in (2.5cm) and 2in (5cm) round and chisel-ended artist's bristle brushes
- Clear wax
- 1in (2.5cm) brush, to apply the wax
- Clean, dry, lint-free cloths, to wipe off the wax

LEFT *It is easier and often more rewarding to work on a surface that is a neutral, mid-tone color, such as cool and soft Duck Egg Blue, then to print deep and light tones on top, such as English Yellow (bright, light, warm, and clear), Burgundy (deep and warm), and Olive (deep and cool).*

1 Using the large, oval brush, paint the surface of the table in Duck Egg Blue. Let it dry.

2 With the artist's brushes, paint your design on a sheet of paper—I did simple Burgundy flowers, with English Yellow centers, and leaves in Olive. Apply the paint thickly but not so thick that it is too wet and won't spread, and not too dry so that it won't be wet enough to print.

3 Place the paper paint-side down on the tabletop, and rub your hand firmly over the paper to make the paint stick to the surface. Lift the paper off immediately. This first print is likely to be light, as the paper will absorb some of the paint.

4 Repeat the process, reapplying paint to the same areas on the paper but printing in a new area on the tabletop, to build up the design. Work fairly quickly, not allowing any drying time, so the paper stays wet. Some of the printed paint on the tabletop from the first printing will transfer to the paper and so mark the second printing.

5 Keep printing to make certain there are no ugly gaps in the design—breathing spaces are fine but not if the surface looks "bald." Let the paint dry.

6 Once the paint has dried, brush on a layer of clear wax with the 1in (2.5cm) brush, wiping it as you go with a clean, dry cloth.

index

acknowledgments

A summer was spent visiting our house in France and working on it after Edward Chalkley had spent the winter making our two new bedrooms, followed by Dino Nuzi "Falemnderit shumë", who, among other finishing touches, plastered the walls with his traditional mud mixture.

The painting team in France mainly comprised Charlotte Freeston who was my right-hand girl (and provider of shoes!), with invaluable help from Valeska Hykel who really got stuck in. Huge thanks to Claire Chalkley for stepping up to the plate at the last minute and for her utterly stunning flowers —and we haven't forgotten the ratatouille! And many thanks to Sam Scott for his skillful carpentry and to Christopher Drake, expert photographer, who also made us laugh.

There was a lovely team of people who helped make it happen, who stayed in Oxford looking after the shop and the paint orders (Cal Dagul, Jane Warnick, Dom Hand, Amy Honour), and others who made curtains and cushions often at the last minute (many thanks Julie), and did upholstery with a quick turn-around (grazie Ricardo) while we were away. Thank you to Kyle Lane whose fabulous plate didn't make it into the book, and to Lizzy Brown and Felix Manuel for being generally helpful, particularly with the final stages of the book. I am also very grateful to Gillian Haslam, my editor, for remaining calm while others—namely me—didn't.

A thousand thanks to all my stockists everywhere who have given me so much support and keep me laughing, and to everyone who I have been inspired by.

And finally to David, for being more than just a chauffeur, xx

Annie

useful addresses

For more information about Annie Sloan Interiors and for a complete list of stockists where you can buy my paint, Chalk Paint®, and other products, please go to www.anniesloan.com.
Charcoal Pastoral from the Annie Sloan Fabric Collection shown on the gilded rococo chair on pages 28–31.

Follow me on
Blog: www.anniesloanpaintandcolour.blogspot.co.uk
Twitter: www.twitter.com/AnnieSloanHome
Pinterest: www.pinterest.com/AnnieSloanHome
YouTube: www.youtube.com/AnnieSloanOfficial
Facebook: www.facebook.com/AnnieSloanHome